WOODCRAFT

of the World

WOODCRAFT

of the World

THUNDER BAY
P·R·E·S·S

First published in the United States 1995
by Thunder Bay Press
5880 Oberlin Drive, Suite 400, San Diego, CA 92121-9653

Publisher: Tracy Marsh
Art Director: Vicki James
Project Coordinator: Debi McCulloch
Editor: Susan Gray
Editorial Assistant: Leonie Draper
Graphic Designer: Peta Nugent
Photographer: Adam Bruzzone
Photographic Stylist: Anne-Maree Unwin
Production Manager: Mick Bagnato

Library of Congress Cataloging-in-Publication Data
Woodcraft of the world / [editor. Leonie A. Draper].
    p.   cm.
  "First published in Australia in 1995 by RD Press" --T.p. verso.
  Includes index.
  ISBN 1-57145-066-1
  1. Woodwork.   I. Draper, Leonie A., 1959-
TT180.W594 1995
674'.8--dc20   95-18367
                                CIP

Manufactured by Mandarin Offset, Hong Kong
Printed in Hong Kong

CONTENTS

ABOUT THIS BOOK

WOOD IS THE PERFECT RAW MATERIAL. It can be shaped and joined, it is durable, strong, and beautiful and can be immensely varied. In countries where timber is plentiful, wood has become an integral part of daily life, with homes, furniture and utensils fashioned out of timber. In other parts of the world, imported wood is reserved for prized possessions. In all communities, the crafting of wood is a valued skill.

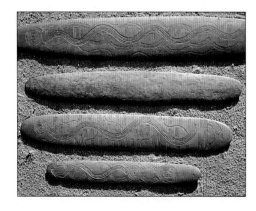

Methods of handling wood vary greatly around the world. People inhabiting remote regions or colonizing new lands often needed to fulfill the roles of forester, carpenter, joiner, as well as many others, and the simplest techniques were preferred. In settled communities where specialist carpenters and joiners were more common, ordinary people turned their hand to decoration: carving spoons as love tokens or toys for children to enjoy.

Rocking horse

Religion and philosophy also affected the way in which wood was crafted. Perfection in construction became a basic tenet held and practiced beautifully by the American Shakers and Japanese woodworkers. The ornate fretwork of the Islamic peoples resulted from religious requirements and a practical need to filter light and air. All cultures developed their own ways of accentuating the natural beauty of the grain and texture in timber and of concealing any flaws.

In today's world of mass-manufacturing and of synthetic materials, a handmade wooden piece is an object of great beauty and a reminder of past values. Whether it is an elaborately carved table or a modest cutlery tray, its individuality gives its owner a sense of pride, to say nothing of the satisfaction gained in the

making of it. We are in the enviable position of being able to pick and choose from the world's wealth of traditions and techniques. This book inspires you to develop your own personal woodcraft style and skills.

Each chapter reviews a different woodcraft tradition including the approach to design, the construction techniques used and popular methods of decoration. The chapter opening page provides insight into the heritage of each culture's style and the effects of local conditions on woodcraft design, technique and finishing. The Designs and Variations spreads offer a wealth of ideas for adapting designs, for alternative timbers and for embellishing the finished pieces. The step-by-step sections guide you through the project construction to produce an article in the style of that tradition. Each project is graded in the following way:

BEGINNER
No woodworking experience required, but you will need to refer to the General Information chapter

INTERMEDIATE
A more demanding project in terms of time and skills; beginners may require help

ADVANCED
Requires patience and a confident hand; may require specialized equipment

Early examples of wooden implements made by Australian Aborigines, featuring ancient designs and patterns.

The General Information chapter explains how to select timber, work the wood and finish your project. A catalogue of timbers is included, listing the main features of each, so that you can select suitable alternatives if necessary. There is a visual cutting list for each project and this contains any patterns required, ready for tracing, enlarging and transferring. Finally, there is a comprehensive glossary and an index to help you locate information you may require, and to enable you to enjoy this book to the full.

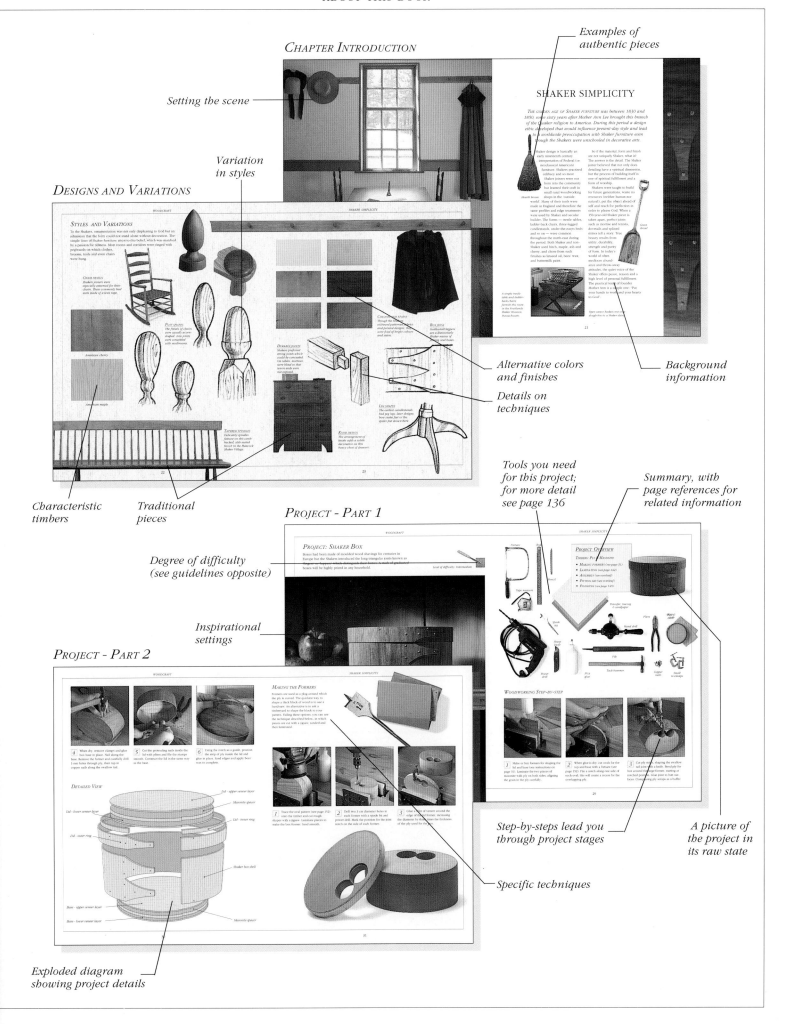

CHAPTER INTRODUCTION

Examples of
authentic pieces

Setting the scene

Variation
in styles

DESIGNS AND VARIATIONS

Alternative colors
and finishes

Background
information

Details on
techniques

Characteristic
timbers

Traditional
pieces

Tools you need
for this project;
for more detail
see page 136

Summary, with
page references for
related information

PROJECT - PART 1

Degree of difficulty
(see guidelines opposite)

Inspirational
settings

PROJECT - PART 2

Step-by-steps lead you
through project stages

A picture of
the project in
its raw state

Specific techniques

Exploded diagram
showing project details

AMERICAN COUNTRY STYLE

THE FURNITURE OF RURAL AMERICA, like that of colonial Australia, is today prized for its spare and functional design. Its attraction lies not in elegant detail or sophisticated decoration, but in the uncomplicated way of life which it recalls and reflects in the use of natural materials and simple design.

The early American colonists brought with them a taste for very heavy Jacobean furniture. This was typically crafted in oak,

Cradle

using turned spindles and mortise and tenon joinery. Colonial homes were very sparsely furnished and many pieces often served multiple purposes: a chest doubled as a bench, settees converted into beds.

Even after the Revolution, American furniture makers adapted designs from Britain and Europe. The Federal style, which flourished from 1795 to 1818, was influenced by the neoclassical movement in Europe. By the end of the seventeenth century, local cabinet-makers were using dovetail joints to fashion a much lighter style of furniture.

In turn, craftspeople working in rural areas simplified the designs of their urban counterparts, choosing certain features which offered a practical advantage and discarding much of the embellishment.

What decoration did exist was generally added in paint rather than woodwork and was often applied to disguise the quality of the timber. Grain painting, the imitation of an expensive timber grain by marking a colored glaze, was popular during the eighteenth century.

Ethnic groups such as the Pennsylvanian Dutch brought a heritage of folk painting and decorated their traditional furniture with bright motifs. The dower chest and *schrank* or wardrobe were pieces which they introduced into the American home.

Other typical items of furniture might include a dry sink, a food safe and a dresser, on which food was prepared or 'dressed.' One major exception to the preference for utility over other considerations was the rocking chair, which was originally made by modifying standard slat-back chairs, and was made popular by early Americans.

Whirligig

This delightful cottage scene depicts the simple elegance of American Country style décor.

The natural grains of the wood are accentuated by shaping and carving.

DESIGNS AND VARIATIONS

American country style is really an amalgam of styles, influenced by the diverse ethnic groups that colonized the nation. It combines the construction techniques of England and Ireland, the decorative traditions of Scandinavia and Germany, and the naive design of the Spanish Mexicans; all modified for life in a new country. Wind-powered toys were developed due to strong religious beliefs which prohibited work and play on Sundays.

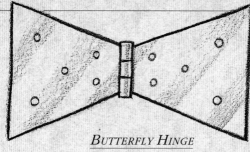

BUTTERFLY HINGE
Surface hinges, like this one, were designed for ornament and function.

DECOYS
This working decoy from the Midwest is weighted with lead.

White ash

Cherry

Maple

Walnut

TIMBERS
By the end of the seventeenth century native timbers such as maple and cherry had replaced imported oak.

WINDSOR CHAIRS
Based on the English design from the town of Windsor, many variations on the basic design were developed throughout America.

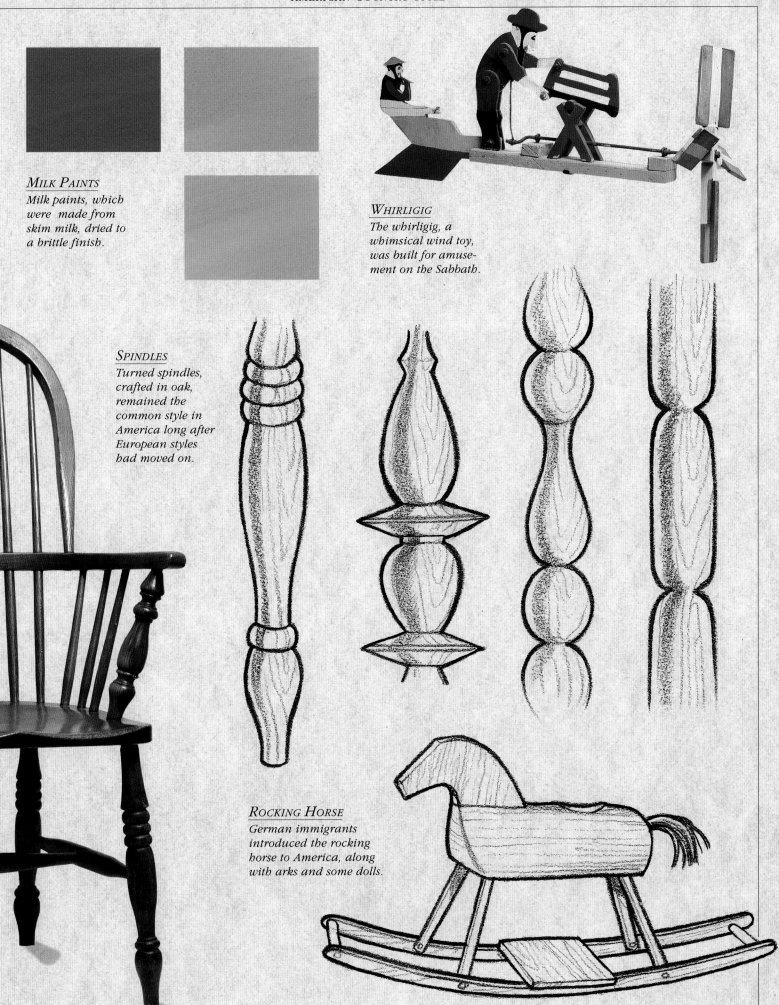

MILK PAINTS
Milk paints, which were made from skim milk, dried to a brittle finish.

WHIRLIGIG
The whirligig, a whimsical wind toy, was built for amusement on the Sabbath.

SPINDLES
Turned spindles, crafted in oak, remained the common style in America long after European styles had moved on.

ROCKING HORSE
German immigrants introduced the rocking horse to America, along with arks and some dolls.

PROJECT: AMERICAN ROCKING HORSE

The rocking horse was one of the most popular toys of the eighteenth and nineteenth centuries. Many rocking horses were built for riding on but this one, based on a turn-of-the-century Pennsylvanian piece, is ornamental rather than practical because of its size.

Level of difficulty: Intermediate

Coping saw   Ruler   Pencil

PROJECT OVERVIEW

TIMBERS: JELUTONG & CHERRY

- LAMINATING (see page 18)
- CARVING (see page 141)
- CHAMFERING (see page 141)
- ASSEMBLY (see below)
- FINISHING (see page 144)

Tracing paper,
Transfer paper
& Sandpaper

Brush

8 x ½ inch
(12 mm)
tacks

Tack
hammer

12 x #4 x ⅝" (20 mm)
round head wood
screws

Glue

Varnish

Brass wire

Leather

Tape
measure

Utility
knife

Paint

Twine

Hand
drill

Whittling knife

Needle-nose
pliers

Screwdriver

Try-square

¾ inch (3/20 mm) gouge

Carver's mallet

WOODWORKING STEP-BY-STEP

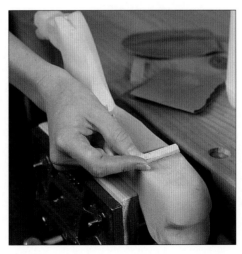

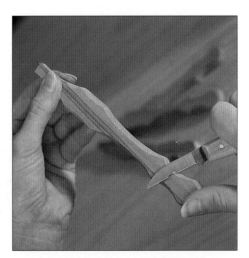

1 Cut timber pieces with a coping saw (see page 149). Sand the gluing surfaces of head and neck smooth, and glue together with body. Carve head, neck and body with chisel and mallet. Sand smooth.

2 Sand a 45° bevel on one edge of the seat back. Glue the seat in position on the horse's back. Using a utility knife, cut the leather reins and saddle to the appropriate sizes (see page 149).

3 Chamfer legs with a whittling knife. Drill screw holes in rockers, spacers, platform and legs. Drill holes ⅝ inch (10 mm) deep into the body to house the legs: drill at an angle of approximately 10° outwards.

4 Assemble the rockers, spacers and platform (see page 15). Attach legs to rockers, leaving screws loose. Glue legs into the body. When glue is dry, tighten the screws attaching legs to rockers.

5 With needle-nose pliers, bend the ends of the brass wire to form loops. Thread each end of the leather rein through a wire loop and glue to secure. Glue the brass bit into horse's mouth.

6 Drill a hole in the horse's rump for the tail. Paint and distress or finish the horse as required. Glue in the twine tail and fray ends to shape. Tack the leather saddle in place to complete.

CARVING

Use a small chisel to carve the detail on the body and head. The carving does not need to be elaborate; simple work will add a primitive charm to the piece. Chamfer the edges of the legs with a whittling knife.

DETAILED VIEW

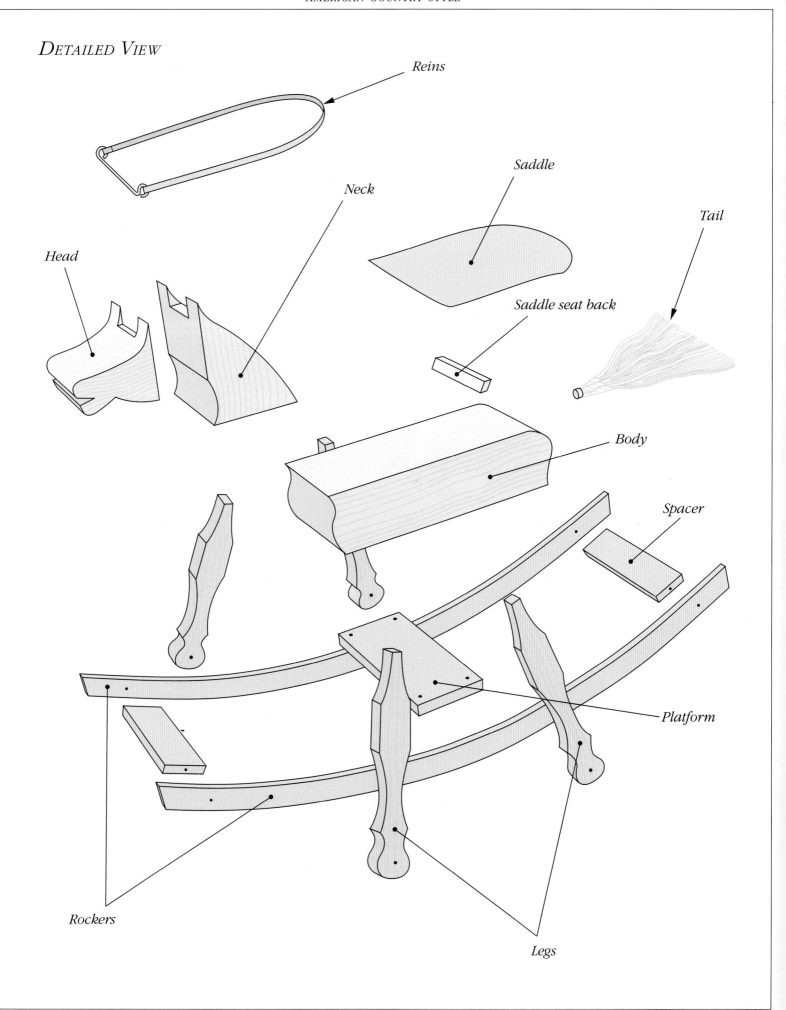

Reins

Saddle

Neck

Tail

Head

Saddle seat back

Body

Spacer

Platform

Rockers

Legs

PROJECT: AMERICAN DOUGH BIN

The making of bread was a part of daily life for most American
households, especially in rural areas. The dough bin was designed
to fulfill several roles in the process: the dough was kneaded on
the stable box top and then placed inside the box to rise.

Level of difficulty: Intermediate

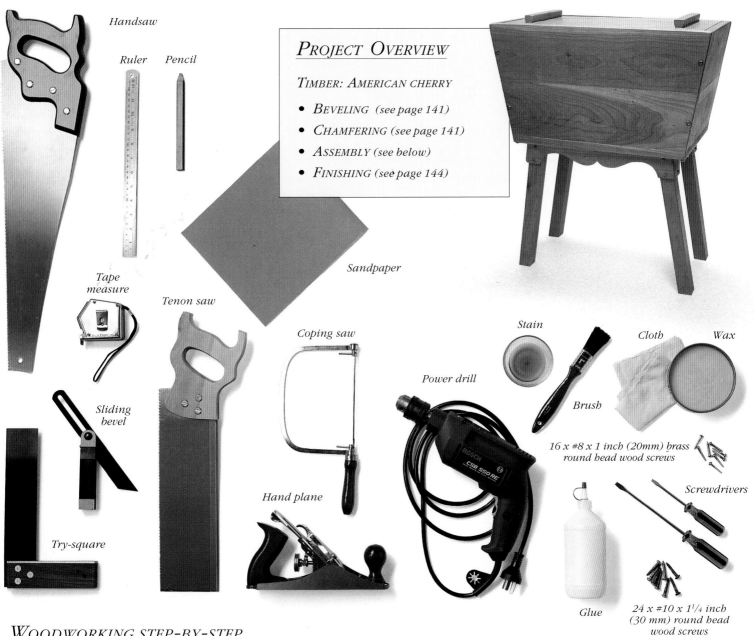

Handsaw

Ruler *Pencil*

PROJECT OVERVIEW

TIMBER: AMERICAN CHERRY

- BEVELING *(see page 141)*
- CHAMFERING *(see page 141)*
- ASSEMBLY *(see below)*
- FINISHING *(see page 144)*

Sandpaper

Tape measure

Tenon saw

Coping saw

Stain

Cloth *Wax*

Power drill

Brush

Sliding bevel

16 x #8 x 1 inch (20mm) brass round head wood screws

Hand plane

Screwdrivers

Try-square

Glue

24 x #10 x 1¼ inch (30 mm) round head wood screws

WOODWORKING STEP-BY-STEP

1 Cut pieces to size. Laminate pieces to form the base, ends, sides and lid. Transfer the pattern (page 150) on to the four skirt pieces and cut with a coping saw.

2 Plane 80° parallel bevels on the edges of the four end pieces and laminate them in pairs. Saw 80° parallel bevels on the top and base of the legs.

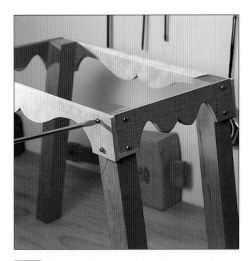

3 Using glue, attach each leg to the inside angle between two of the skirt pieces until all legs and skirts are joined. Secure with two screws at each leg.

4 Assemble the box sides and ends and secure with screws along the edges of the sides. Screw the base on to the sides. Glue legs and skirts to the base.

5 Cut the lid handles and shape them with a hand plane. Glue the handles on to the lid piece, narrow edges down, at equal distances from the ends.

6 Bevel the ends of the four cleats and test that the lid will rest evenly on them. Glue cleats in position as shown. Sand all surfaces and wax to complete.

LAMINATING

When making items such as table-tops and box sides, pieces of wood are glued together in a process known as laminating. To achieve a successfully glued join, the edges of the timber must be perfectly flat and at 90° to the faces. Spread the glue evenly and sparingly over the edges (follow the glue manufacturer's instructions for preparation etc.) and lightly clamp together with a bar clamp. Ensure the boards are sitting flat and allow to dry. Overtightening the clamp may cause the wood to buckle.

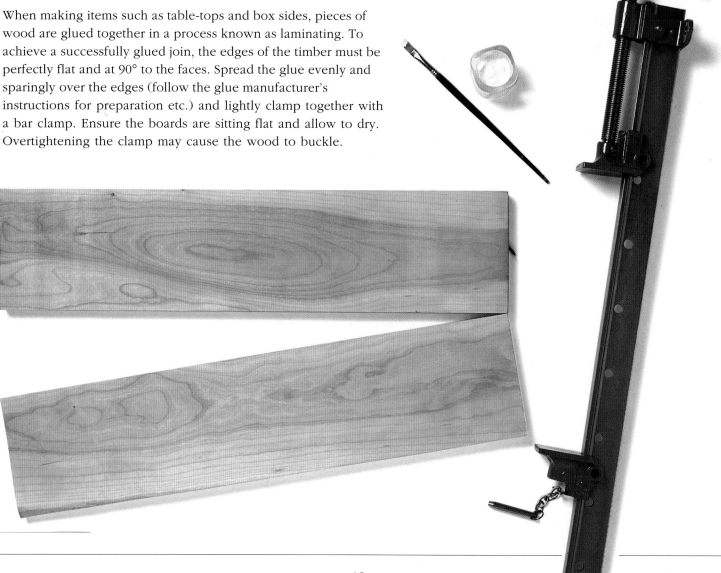

DETAILED VIEW

Handles

Lid

Sides

Cleats

End

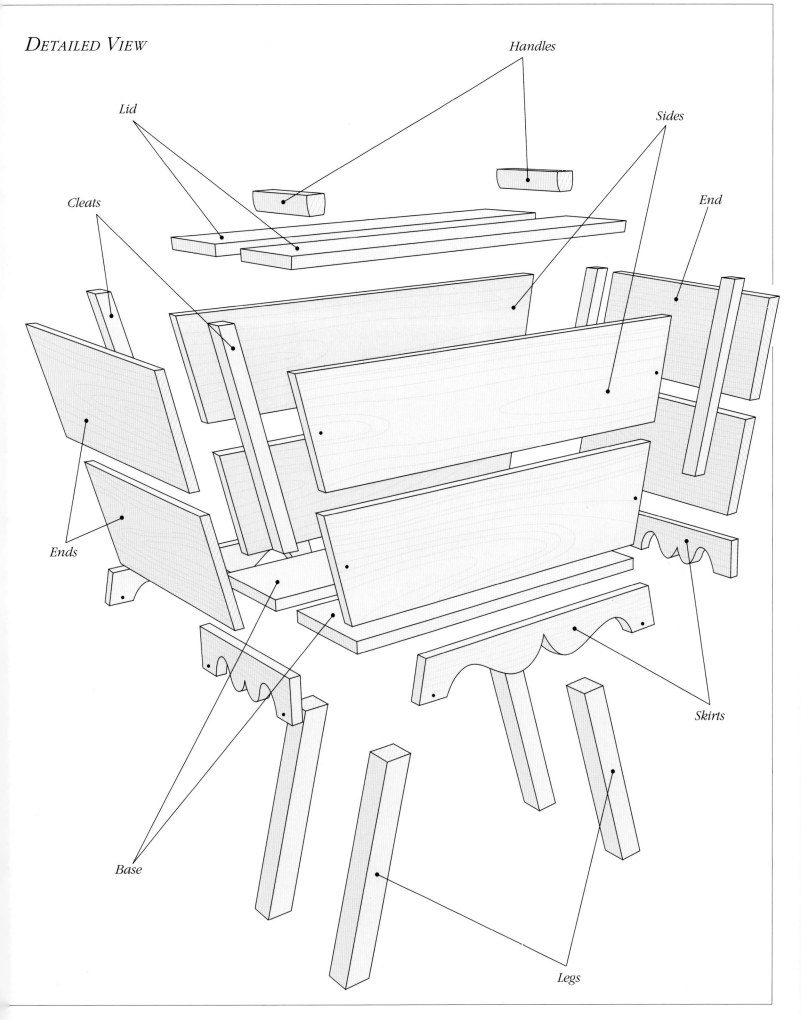

Ends

Skirts

Base

Legs

SHAKER SIMPLICITY

THE GOLDEN AGE OF SHAKER FURNITURE was between 1830 and 1850, some sixty years after Mother Ann Lee brought this branch of the Quaker religion to America. During this period a design ethic developed that would influence present-day style and lead to a worldwide preoccupation with Shaker furniture even though the Shakers were unschooled in decorative arts.

Shaker design is basically an early nineteenth century interpretation of Federal (or neoclassical American) furniture. Shakers practiced celibacy, and so most Shaker joiners were not born into the community but learned their craft in small rural woodworking shops in the 'outside world.' Many of their tools were made in England and, therefore, the same profiles and edge treatments were used by Shaker and secular builders. The forms — trestle tables, ladder-back chairs, three-legged candlestands, under-the-eaves beds and so on — were common throughout the North-east during the period. Both Shaker and non-Shaker used birch, maple, ash and cherry, and chose from finishes such as linseed oil, bees' wax, and buttermilk paint.

Hearth broom

So if the material, form and finish are not uniquely Shaker, what is? The answer is the detail. The Shaker joiner believed that not only does detailing have a spiritual dimension, but the process of building itself is one of spiritual fulfilment and a form of worship.

Shakers were taught to build for future generations, waste no resources (neither human nor natural), put the object ahead of self and reach for perfection in order to please God. When a 150 year-old Shaker piece is taken apart, perfect joints such as mortise and tenons, dovetails and splined miters, reveal the close attention they paid to detail. Their true beauty results from the durability, utility, strength and purity of form. In today's world of often mediocre abundance and throw-away attitudes, working in the Shaker style offers tranquil simplicity and a high degree of personal fulfilment. The practical tenet of founder Mother Ann is a simple one: "Put your hands to work and your hearts to God."

Grain shovel

A simple trestle table and ladder-back chairs furnish this room in the Fruitlands Shaker Museum, Massachusetts.

Open weave baskets rest on a dough bin in a Shaker dairy.

STYLES AND VARIATIONS

To the Shakers, ornamentation was not only displeasing to God but an admission that the form could not stand alone without decoration. The simple lines of Shaker furniture attest to this belief, which was matched by a passion for tidiness. Most rooms and corridors were ringed with pegboards on which clothes, brooms, tools and even chairs were hung.

CHAIR DESIGN
Shaker joiners were especially esteemed for their chairs. These commonly had seats made of woven tape.

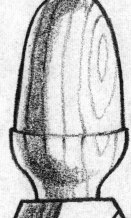

American cherry

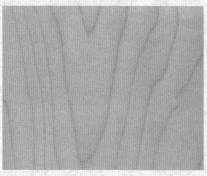

American maple

FINIAL SHAPES
The finials of chairs were usually acorn-shaped. Arm joints were concealed with mushrooms.

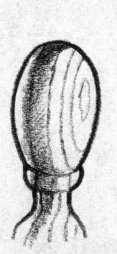

TAPERED SPINDLES
Delicate spindles are featured on this comb-backed, slab-seated bench in the Hancock Shaker Village.

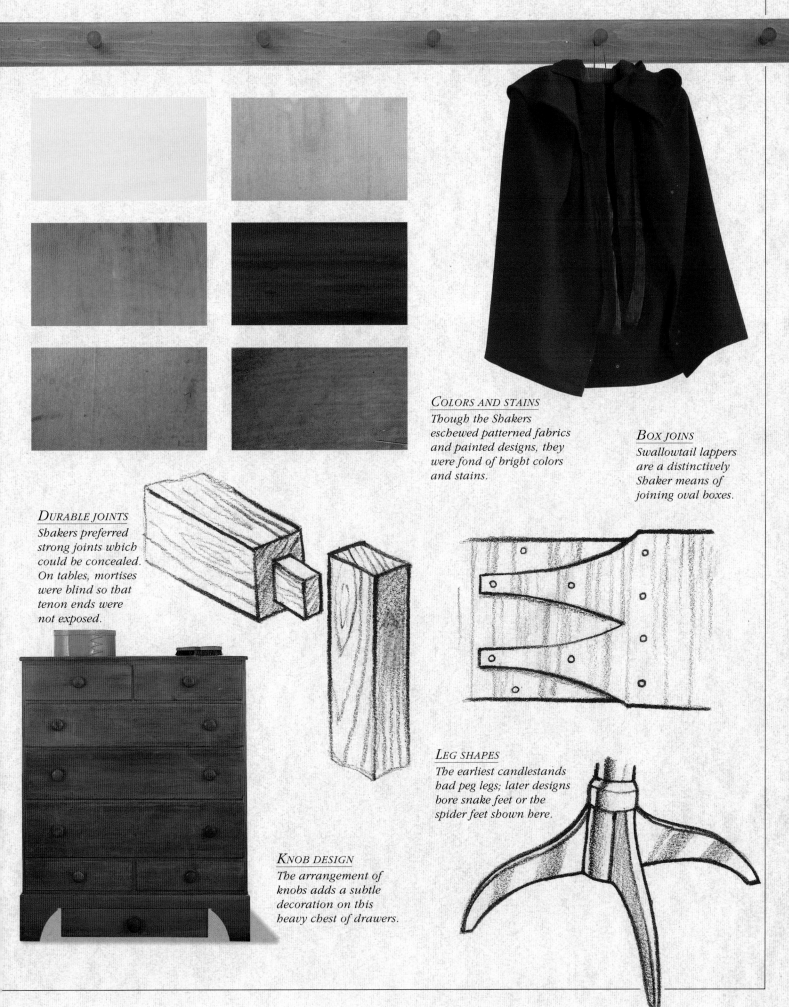

COLORS AND STAINS
Though the Shakers eschewed patterned fabrics and painted designs, they were fond of bright colors and stains.

BOX JOINS
Swallowtail lappers are a distinctively Shaker means of joining oval boxes.

DURABLE JOINTS
Shakers preferred strong joints which could be concealed. On tables, mortises were blind so that tenon ends were not exposed.

LEG SHAPES
The earliest candlestands had peg legs; later designs bore snake feet or the spider feet shown here.

KNOB DESIGN
The arrangement of knobs adds a subtle decoration on this heavy chest of drawers.

PROJECT: SHAKER CANDLESTAND

Three-legged candlestands and sewing tables were made in each of the Shaker communities with variations. This one has snake feet and a hexagonal post connected with mortise and tenon joints, dovetail joints were more commonly used but they are more involved.

Level of difficulty: Advanced

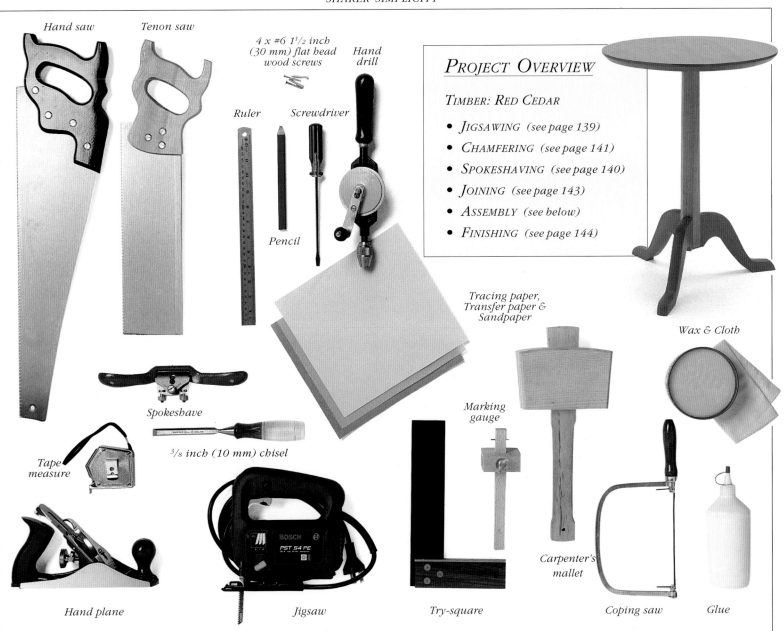

Hand saw   Tenon saw

4 x #6 1¹/₂ inch
(30 mm) flat head
wood screws   Hand
drill

Ruler   Screwdriver

Pencil

Spokeshave

Tape
measure

³/₈ inch (10 mm) chisel

Hand plane   Jigsaw   Try-square

Tracing paper,
Transfer paper &
Sandpaper

Marking
gauge

Wax & Cloth

Carpenter's
mallet

Coping saw   Glue

PROJECT OVERVIEW

TIMBER: RED CEDAR

- **JIGSAWING** (see page 139)
- **CHAMFERING** (see page 141)
- **SPOKESHAVING** (see page 140)
- **JOINING** (see page 143)
- **ASSEMBLY** (see below)
- **FINISHING** (see page 144)

WOODWORKING STEP-BY-STEP

1 Trace leg pattern (page 151) so that length runs along grain. Cut the profiles with a jigsaw. Mark and cut a ¹/₂ x ¹/₂ inch (12 x 12 mm) tenon full-width on each leg.

2 Use a spokeshave to round off the outside of each leg, except for the convex section, which you will not be able to reach with the spokeshave blade.

3 Sand the convex section of the legs. Cut the pedestal with a handsaw. Cut the doughnut using a jigsaw and the plate using a coping saw.

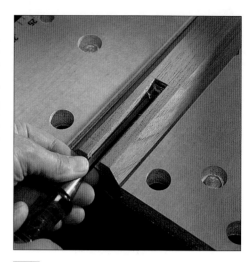

4 Laminate top and profile. Draw a 18³/10 inch (465 mm) radius circle on underside. On rim, scribe a line ⁵/16 inch (7 mm) from top. Chamfer edge to lines using spokeshave.

5 Use a hand plane to plane the table pedestal so that it is hexagonal and so that it tapers from a 2⁹/16 inch (65 mm) diameter at the base to a 2 inch (50 mm) diameter at the top.

6 Mark three evenly spaced mortises in the base of the pedestal with a scribe. Using a chisel and mallet, cut each of the mortises ¹/2 x ¹/2 inch (12 x 12 mm) deep.

7 Draw a 2 inch (50 mm) hexagon in the center of the doughnut. Chisel a hole ¹/16 inch (1 mm) smaller than the hexagon and sand the hole back to the marked lines.

8 Insert the legs into the pedestal and test that the table is level. Glue all the legs in place. Glue the plate so that it conceals the base of the pedestal.

9 Glue and then screw the doughnut in position on the table-top. Glue the pedestal into the doughnut. Sand to a smooth finish and wax to complete.

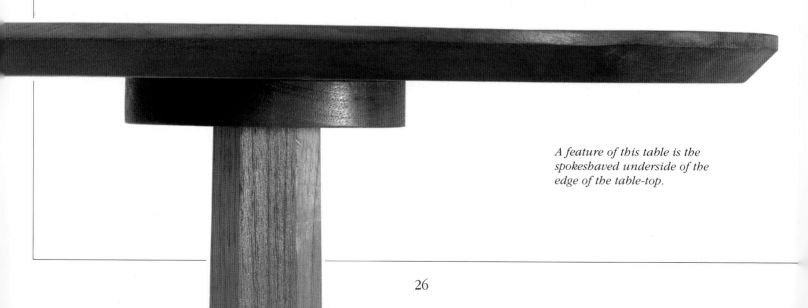

A feature of this table is the spokeshaved underside of the edge of the table-top.

DETAILED VIEW

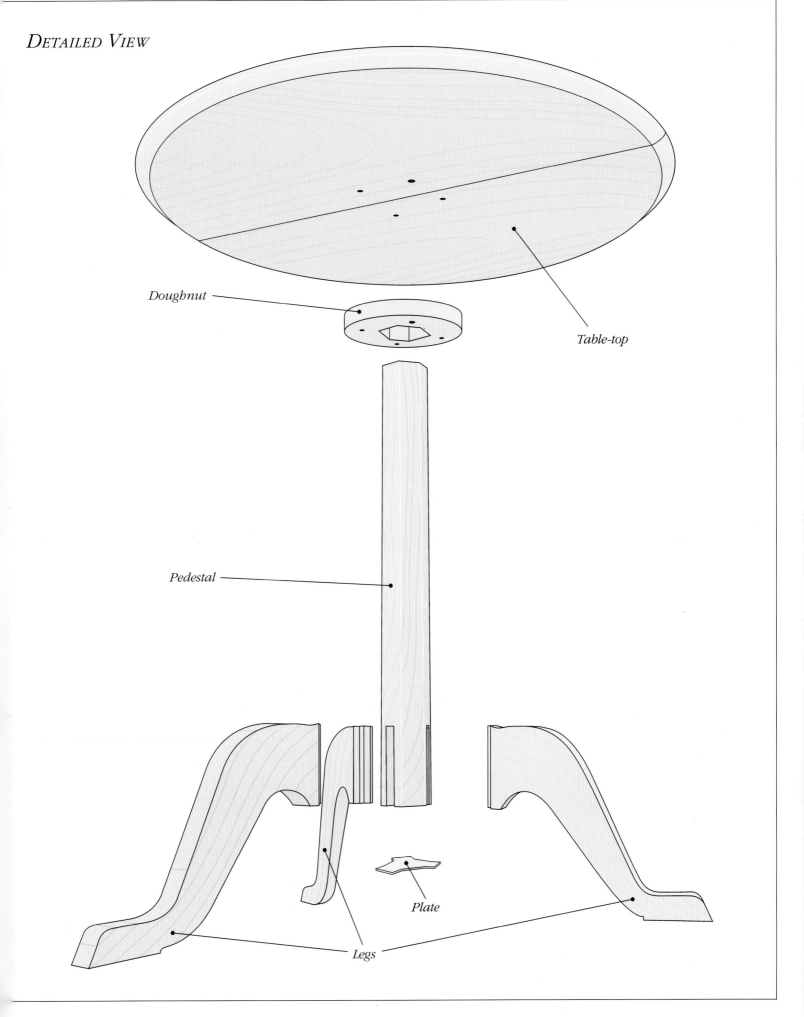

Doughnut

Table-top

Pedestal

Plate

Legs

PROJECT: SHAKER BOX

Boxes had been made of molded wood shavings for centuries in
Europe, but the Shakers introduced the long, triangular joints known
as 'fingers' or 'lappers' which distinguish their boxes. A stack of
graduated boxes will be highly prized in any household.

Level of difficulty: Advanced

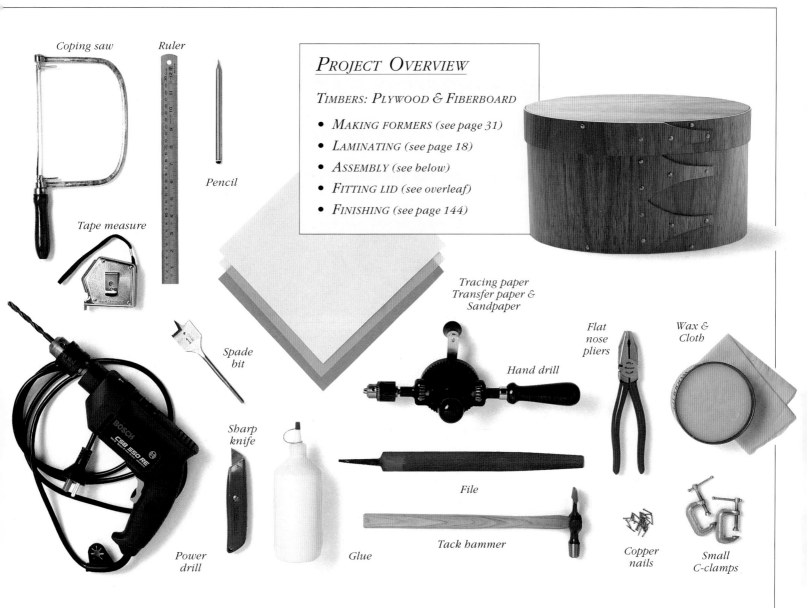

Coping saw

Ruler

Pencil

Tape measure

PROJECT OVERVIEW

TIMBERS: PLYWOOD & FIBERBOARD

- MAKING FORMERS (*see page 31*)
- LAMINATING (*see page 18*)
- ASSEMBLY (*see below*)
- FITTING LID (*see overleaf*)
- FINISHING (*see page 144*)

Tracing paper
Transfer paper &
Sandpaper

Spade bit

Sharp knife

Hand drill

Flat nose pliers

Wax & Cloth

File

Power drill

Glue

Tack hammer

Copper nails

Small C-clamps

WOODWORKING STEP-BY-STEP

1 Make or buy formers for shaping the lid and base (see instructions on page 31). Laminate the pieces of fiberboard for the lid and base with plywood on each side, with the plywood grain running lengthwise.

2 When the glue is dry, cut the ovals for the top and base (see page 152) with a coping saw. File a notch along one side of each oval (see page 140); this will create a recess to house the overlapping plywood.

3 Cut plywood strips, shaping the swallowtail joint with a knife. Bend box plywood around the large former starting at notched position. Glue surfaces and butt joint. Clamp until dry using plywood scraps to buffer.

4 Remove clamps and glue in the box base. Nail along base. Remove the former and drill ¹/₈ inch (3 mm) holes through ply, tap in copper nails along the swallow tail.

5 Cut the protruding nails inside the lid with the pliers and file back the stumps till flush with surface. Construct the lid in the same way as the base.

6 Using the notch as a guide, position the strip of plywood inside the lid and glue in place. Sand all the edges and apply bees' wax to finish the timber.

DETAILED VIEW

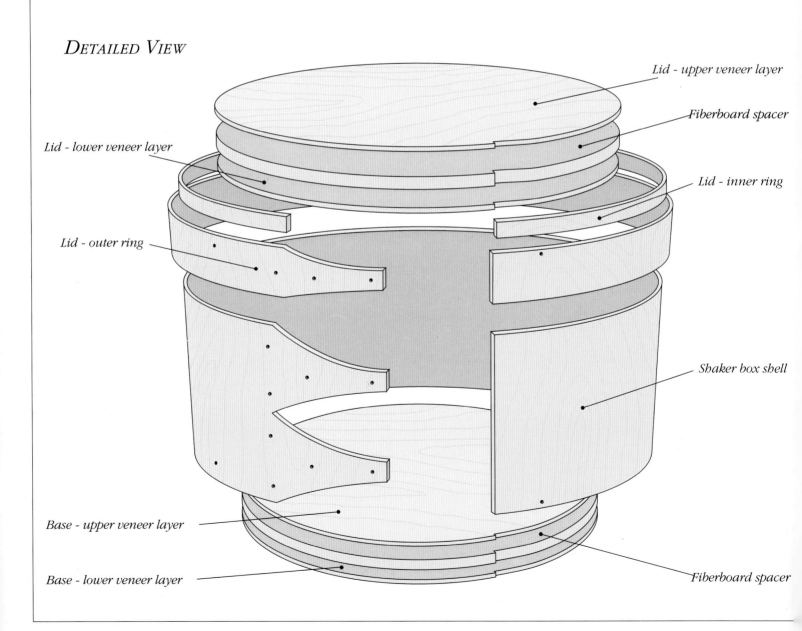

Lid - upper veneer layer

Fiberboard spacer

Lid - lower veneer layer

Lid - inner ring

Lid - outer ring

Shaker box shell

Base - upper veneer layer

Base - lower veneer layer

Fiberboard spacer

MAKING THE FORMERS

Formers are used as a plug around which the plywood is curved. The quickest way to shape a thick block of wood is to use a band-saw. An alternative is to ask a timber yard to shape the block to your pattern. Failing these options, you can use the technique described below, in which pieces are cut with a jigsaw, sanded and then laminated.

1 Trace the oval pattern (see page 152) on to the timber and cut rough shapes with a jigsaw. Laminate pieces to make the box former. Sand smooth.

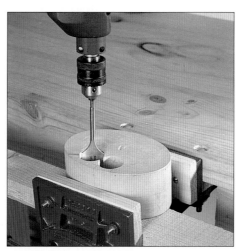

2 Drill two 1³/₈ inch (3 cm) diameter holes in each former with a spade bit and power drill. Mark the position for the joint notch on the side of each former.

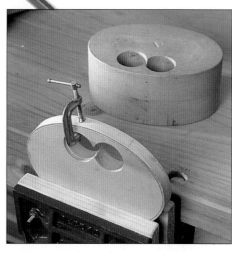

3 Glue a fillet of veneer around the edge of the lid former, increasing the diameter by three times the thickness of the plywood used for the box.

WOODCRAFT OF SCANDINAVIA

IN THE COLD COUNTRIES of northern Europe timber has traditionally been the major resource, the complete provider for the people. In Scandinavia, where wood has been used for anything and everything from grand churches to the tiny needles of lacemakers, woodworking is both an art and a craft.

The ancient Viking boats were constructed to withstand the freezing oceans, but much artistic expression was wrought into the wood as well: homage to a god in a carved prow, or some decoration to please the eyes of humans. The medieval stave churches are filled with masterful detail, from the wooden shingles overhead to the intricately carved doors. Traditionally, the major part of every Scandinavian home was made out of timber, which was used in the construction and lining as well as in the furnishings. The joinery and details vary from one part of Scandinavia to another, affected by the properties of the timber being worked.

Viking chair

The long fibers of hardwoods—the ashes, oaks and beeches commonly found in Denmark and the birches of Finland—allow for extremely fine and elegant detail. The pines of Sweden and Norway dictate a bigger and heavier style.

Eating, drinking and many other domestic activities in a Scandinavian home would be well served by utensils made from wood. Commonly, the household's collection of plates and bowls were displayed on railed wooden shelves high up on the walls. With the emphasis on practicality, the woodware would be leaned forward to prevent dust and soot from collecting. Joined wedding spoons, with which a bride and groom would eat together at their marriage feast, were carved from a single piece of wood and proudly displayed in the home of the newlywed couple.

In the Scandinavian approach, things made of wood cannot merely be practical. Each piece must have its own beauty in shape, design and decoration. In this way the people of Scandinavia pay tribute to the forests which have sustained them so well over the centuries.

Wedding spoon

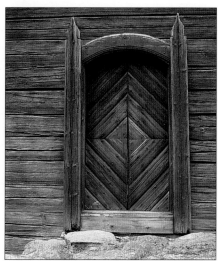

Timber—carved, shaped, painted, or unadorned—furnishes this room in a Scandinavian farmhouse.

Rough hewn and mitered planks are arranged to form a geometric pattern.

DESIGNS AND VARIATIONS

Scandinavia comprises several countries, and diversity is apparent in the woodcraft of the different regions. The people of Finland and Sweden tend to practice a discipline of strict proportion and plain lines. The Norwegians draw on the richness of Viking tradition and use paint and carving to ornament furniture and architectural detail. Rough-hewn or smooth, Scandinavian style is always graceful.

BUTTER MOLD
This intricately carved and hinged box serves simply to impress a pattern on to home-churned butter.

KUBBESTOL
This traditional chair is made from a single hollowed log.

SAUNA BUCKETS
Wooden buckets are used for rinsing after bathing and for ladling water on to hot rocks.

CHAIR DETAIL
Carvings on the arms and boss add interest to an already majestic form.

VIKING CARVING
The intricate designs of the Vikings were dominated by elaborate scrollwork.

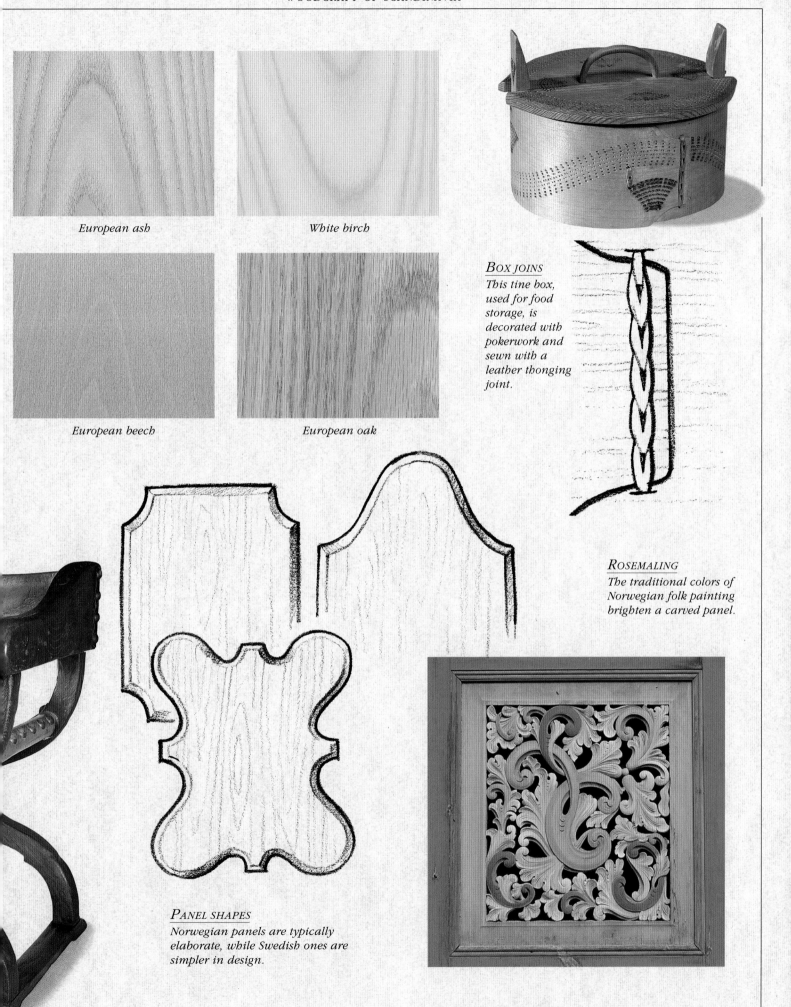

European ash

White birch

European beech

European oak

BOX JOINS
This tine box, used for food storage, is decorated with pokerwork and sewn with a leather thonging joint.

ROSEMALING
The traditional colors of Norwegian folk painting brighten a carved panel.

PANEL SHAPES
Norwegian panels are typically elaborate, while Swedish ones are simpler in design.

PROJECT: SCANDINAVIAN WALL CUPBOARD

Wall cupboards are found throughout all of the Scandinavian countries, although
the shapes of pediments and door plaques vary. This cupboard has been made
using the simplest methods of construction; hence it is not really as ambitious
as it might appear and as the finished cupboard might suggest.

Level of difficulty: Advanced

Handsaw

Ruler

Pencil

Tracing paper
Transfer paper &
Sandpaper

Tape
measure

PROJECT OVERVIEW

TIMBER: BALTIC PINE

- LAMINATING (see page 142)
- ROUTING (see page 139)
- ASSEMBLY (see below)
- PROFILING (see page 140)
- ATTACHING HINGES (see overleaf)
- FINISHING (see page 144)

Jigsaw

Brush

Paint

Screwdriver

Wax &
Cloth

Flat head
screws for
hinges

Dowels

Two hinges

Door lock

Brads

8d (45 mm)
finish nails

Router

Hand plane

Power drill

Glue

Hammer

WOODWORKING STEP-BY-STEP

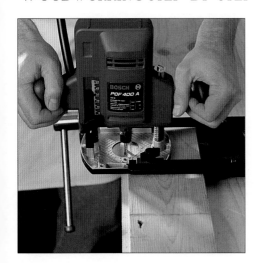

1 Cut pieces to size (see page 153). Laminate backing and panel pieces. Rout a ⅜ x ½ inch (10 x 12 mm) rabbet on sides, top and base. Or backing can be attached flush.

2 Assemble the cupboard (see page 39) and fix in position using the bullet head nails. Nail the support strips in position and insert the two shelves.

3 Glue the door frame together, and clamp in place until the glue is dry. Drill holes at each of the joints and insert the glued dowels to hold (see page 72).

4 Transfer the pattern for the panel and profile with a jigsaw. Chamfer the edges with sandpaper. Attach the panel to the door with brads.

5 Attach hinges to the inside of the door and screw the door onto the body of the cupboard. Attach the door handle using a 2 inch (50 mm) screw.

6 Profile the pediment with the jigsaw and then nail it to the top of the cupboard. Sand and finish by liming and applying bees' wax.

LIMING

This is a technique which adds depth to the appearance of the finished piece. A thinned paint is applied to the surface and then allowed to dry slightly before being wiped off with a damp sponge or a dry brush. Any damaging should be done before liming so that traces of color will lodge in the indentations. Always wipe from the center of the surface in the direction of the grain. For a deeper color apply a second coat of liming or leave the paint to dry longer. To lighten the color, wipe the surface over with the appropriate solvent.

Detailed View

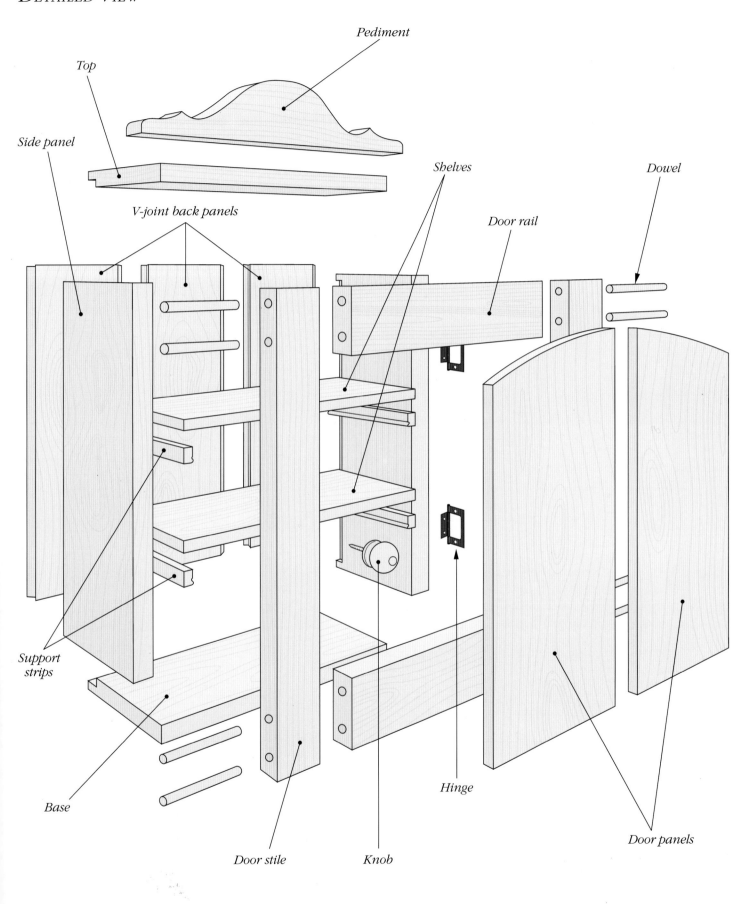

Pediment

Top

Side panel

Shelves

Dowel

V-joint back panels

Door rail

Support
strips

Base

Door stile

Knob

Hinge

Door panels

PROJECT: SCANDINAVIAN CHAIR

Nordic peasant furniture of the eighteenth century was quite primitive in design, and traditional chair shapes were no exception. The simple lines of this project, with its elegantly curved backrest, octagonal legs and the pastel treatment of the timber, give it a fresh, Scandinavian feel.

Level of difficulty: Advanced

Carpenter's mallet

Pencil   Ruler

Marking gauge

Tape measure

Sandpaper

Chisels

$1^3/_8$ inch (3 cm) Spade bit

Jigsaw

Hand plane

Power drill

Hammer

Varnish   Brush   Screwdriver

Paint

Glue

Coping saw

Rasp

File

$6 x \#8 x$ $1^1/_4$ inch flat head wood screws

Sliding bevel

PROJECT OVERVIEW

TIMBER: RADIATA PINE

- PROFILING (see page 140)
- JOINING (see page 143)
- ASSEMBLY (see below)
- FINISHING (see page 144)

WOODWORKING STEP-BY-STEP

1 Laminate the two pieces to form the seat. Transfer the pattern (page 154) and cut the seat and backrest with a jigsaw. Drill a large hole in the backrest and jigsaw the cut-out. Rasp and sand smooth.

2 Mark a long tenon at the base of the backrest with a marking gauge, then fashion the tenon with a chisel and mallet. Bevel the tenon to ensure that the backrest will meet the seat at an 80° angle.

3 Fashion an 80° mortise in the seat using a chisel and a mallet. Use a sliding bevel to establish the correct angle. File and sand the mortise back to a very smooth finish (see page 140).

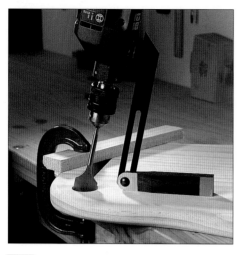

4 Rasp, file and sand the seat edges to round all corners. Use a spade bit to drill leg holes in the seat: the back two holes at 70° and the front two at 80°.

5 Plane the corners of the legs to make them octagonal. Rasp one end of each leg to fit snugly into seat holes. Bevel the base of each leg to suit its position.

6 Align the grain of each leg with the seat and mark a line across the top of the leg. Remove the leg and saw an incision 1³/₁₆ inch (30 mm) deep for the wedge.

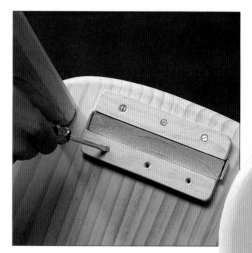

7 Cover the rasped end of each leg with glue and insert in seat hole. Place a wedge in the incision and hammer down to secure the leg. Remove each leg projection with a hand plane.

8 Drill screw holes for the support pieces on the underside of the seat. Insert the backrest into the seat and drive a wedge in at either edge of the tenon to · secure the backrest in position.

9 Bevel the two support pieces so they both fit neatly against the tenon. Glue them in place and screw to secure. Pickle, antique and varnish as required to complete (see below).

PICKLING

Light-colored timbers such as pine can be given an effective pale finish known as pickling. Dampen the raw wood with a cloth. Apply a pickling solution (or a mixture of white paint and sealer) with a large brush and wipe off the excess with a soft, clean cloth.

DETAILED VIEW

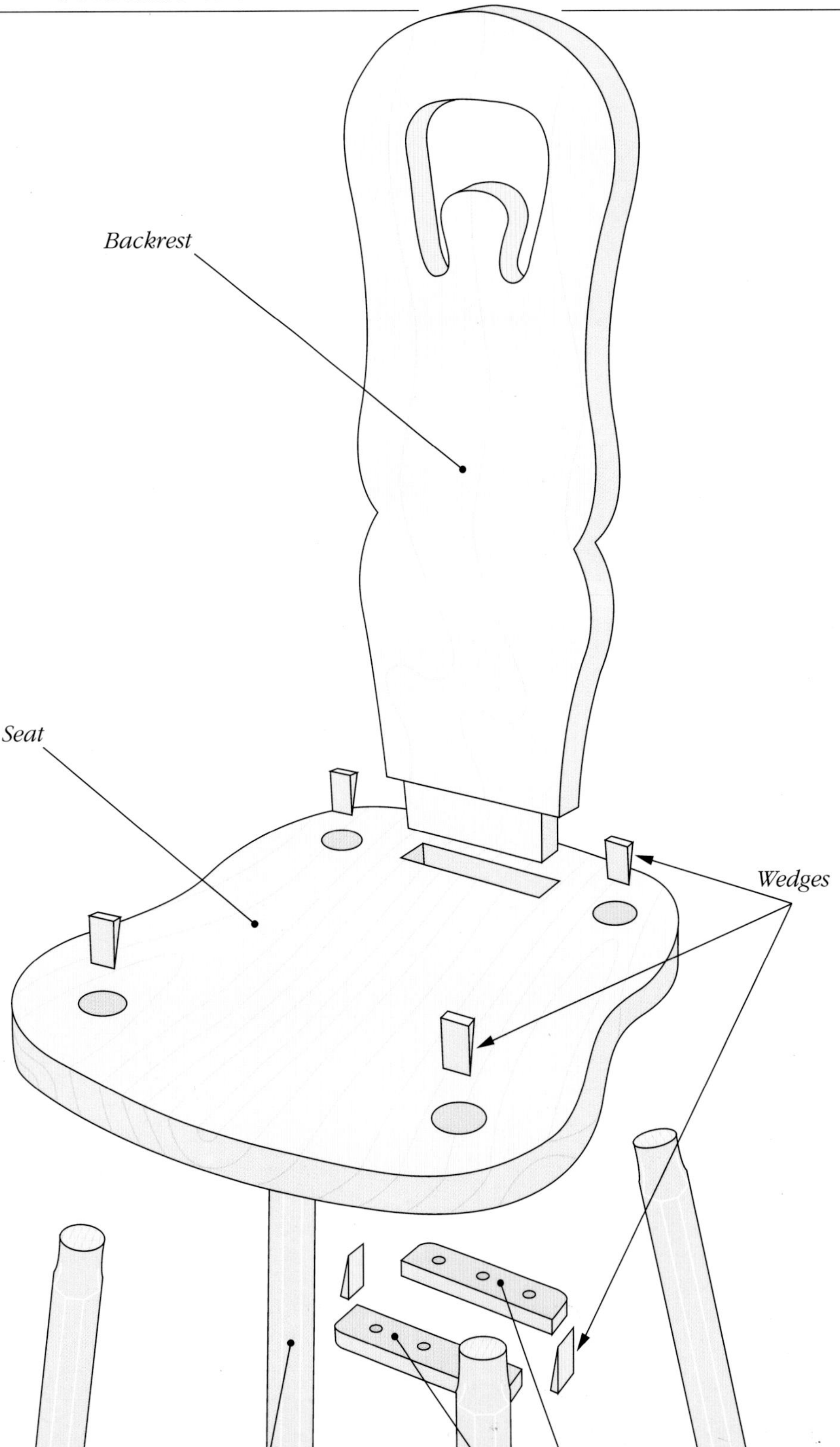

Backrest

Seat

Wedges

Legs

Support strips

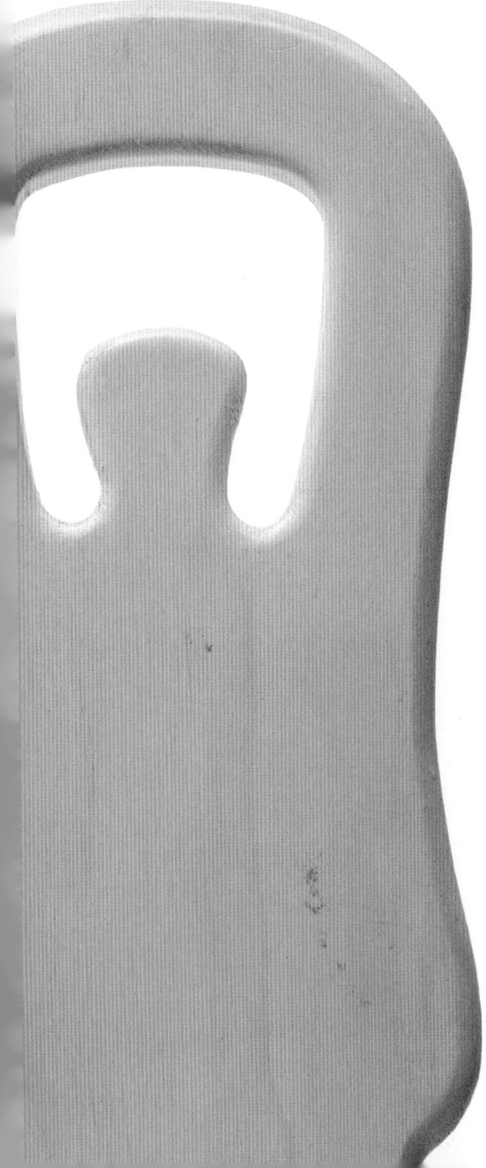

FRENCH PROVINCIAL FURNITURE

IN RECENT TIMES there has been much interest in the traditional furniture of provincial France, a style developed during the reign of Louis XV. Classic shapes such as the cabriole leg, sculpted bouquets, rosettes, rocaille and graceful moldings are our inheritance from this rich tradition.

Butter mold

The printing of manuals and engravings provided French cabinet-makers with patterns for furniture design and encouraged a degree of uniformity. The system of guilds and apprenticeships must also have contributed to this. Guilds had a very strict control over the proficiency of members, a factor which ensured a high quality of workmanship in city and country.

Nonetheless, decoration and design varied greatly from region to region. We find them very graceful, delicate and florid in Lorraine, Normandy and Provence. They are simple and sober in Poiton, Picardy and Champagne; in Burgundy and in the Lyonnais they verge on nobility. But by comparison, in the mountainous regions of Auvergne and Gascony, in coastal Brittany and the *pays* Basque, furniture design is quite primitive and naive.

Most regions produced such pieces as the *armoire*, an ancestor of the wardrobe, chests or *coffres*, and the functional kitchen dresser. The Breton *lit clos*, literally "closed bed," is an example of a regional speciality. Timbers certainly varied depending on availability: harbor areas made use of imported pines, ebony and mahogany. Locally grown oak was often tinted with wax and varnish to take on the color and patina of mahogany. Walnut, chestnut and fruit woods, such as cherry and pear, were also popular for furniture making.

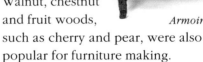

Armoire

Decoration ranged from simple lozenges to ornate carved motifs. Marquetry, *clontage* (embellishment with copper nails) and pokerwork were sometimes added for effect. Paint was applied over inexpensive timber, either in one color or in polychrome which highlighted the carved detail. Furniture was seldom left totally unadorned: shapely moldings added a finishing touch to otherwise plain pieces.

Coffee grinders and other wooden implements fill this cabinet in a French kitchen.

Distressed and gilded paintwork.

DESIGNS AND VARIATIONS

Shaping and carving played an important role in the design of French provincial furniture. Decoration ranged from simple geometric designs such as lozenges, stars or rosettes, to elaborate garlands and acanthus scrolls. Marquetry was another favored technique: many pieces are embellished with small stars in two or three tones of wood. However, French provincial style is not characterized by detail alone; the shape of a piece also reveals its origin.

HINGES
Armoires with rabbeted doors commonly used hinges with a decorative finial.

TABLE DESIGN
This low table is a possible variation for the project in this chapter. Both feature cabriole legs and carving on the skirts.

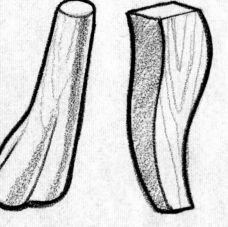

LEG SHAPES
The graceful curve of the cabriole leg is a typical feature, but there are many variations in the foot design.

FABRICS
Blue and white are characteristic colors used in French provincial fabric design.

LIMING
Washing new timber with a thinned coat of white or pastel paint adds a subtle decoration.

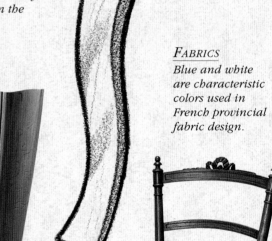

TIMBERS
Other popular timbers included fruit woods such as pearwood and cherry. In southern France, olive and lime were also used.

European oak

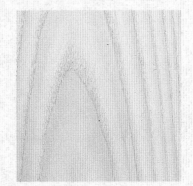

European ash

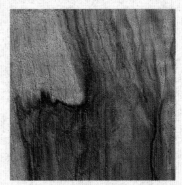

Walnut

KNOBS
Even the plainest chest of drawers is decorated with a simple molding.

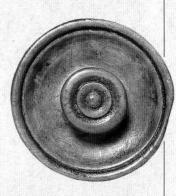

FLORAL DESIGNS
A bouquet escaping from an urn or basket often appears as a sculpted relief on furniture.

STYLE
The combination of curved legs, carved motif and decorated seat make a classic French statement.

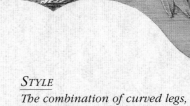

CLASSIC MOTIFS
Scrolls and rocaille, stylized shells, appear on more intricately carved pieces.

PROJECT: PROVINCIAL GRAPE BASKET

Wooden baskets with tapered sides are used by grape-pickers in the Dordogne region of France, while those in other districts prefer plaited baskets worn on the back. Handles are made from whatever is available: thick grapevine, a strong branch or sturdy cane.

Level of difficulty: Beginner

Handsaw

Ruler

Pencil

PROJECT OVERVIEW

TIMBER: BALTIC PINE

- CHAMFERING (see page 141)
- ASSEMBLY (see below)
- FINISHING (see page 144)

Brush

Wax

Sandpaper

Stain

Tape measure

24 x #6 x 1¼ inch brass flat head wood screws

Cloth

Hand plane

small countersink bit

Sliding bevel

Screwdriver

Hand drill

WOODWORKING STEP-BY-STEP

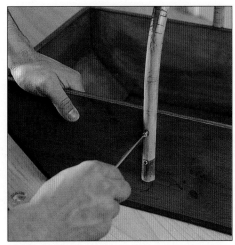

1 Cut all pieces to size (see page 155). Hand plane a 45° bevel along both edges of the two lower end pieces. Use a sliding bevel to check the angle.

2 Mark holes for the screws on the ends and the base. Drill the holes, countersink, and screw pieces together. Chamfer the corners of each edge.

3 Rabbet ends of cane to fit box sides. Soak and bend cane to form handle. Attach with two screws at each side. Sand, stain and wax to complete the piece.

PROJECT: FRENCH PROVINCIAL TABLE

The cabriole legs and graceful proportions of this side table are characteristic
of the French provincial style. Once constructed, the table is heavily
damaged with a sharp object to give it the dents and scratches which imply
that it has already enjoyed a long and eventful life.

Level of difficulty: Advanced

Bar clamp

Ruler Pencil

Tape measure

Sandpaper

PROJECT OVERVIEW

TIMBER: OREGON FIR

- PROFILING *(see page 140)*
- ROUTING *(see page 139)*
- JOINING *(see page 142)*
- CARVING *(see page 141)*
- DAMAGING *(see page 96)*
- ASSEMBLY *(see below)*
- FINISHING *(see page 144)*

Stain   Brush

Wax & Cloth

C-clamps

Carpenter's chisels

Half brick

Carving chisels

Varnish

Dowels

Screwdriver

Carver's mallet

Spokeshave

Doweling jig

Screws & table-top clips

Router

Jigsaw

Power drill

Glue

Carpenter's mallet

Orbital sander

WOODWORKING STEP-BY-STEP

1 Cut timber to size (see page 156), ensuring that the grain matches on each of the legs (see overleaf). Transfer patterns. Mark and drill dowel holes on two inside faces of each leg and on rails.

2 Profile the rails using a jigsaw (see page 140). Use the router to make a ¹/₄ x ¹/₄ inch (6 x 6 mm) groove along the top edge of each of the rails. The routed groove will be used to house the table-top clips.

3 Use a bandsaw to profile legs (see overleaf for more detail). If you do not have a bandsaw available, then use a spokeshave or a draw knife to shape the legs. Sand smooth with an orbital sander.

4 Profile the table-top using either a jigsaw or a bandsaw. Then use a router to rout the molding along the edge of the table-top, which is for decoration.

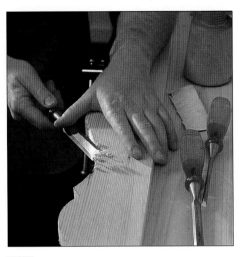

5 First carve the skirt, then chamfer the edge with a chisel. Once you have done this, use some fine grade sandpaper to round off the edges.

6 Using a sharp pencil or a knife, mark a line approximately ¼ inch (6 mm) in from the edge of the skirt. Use the chisel to dig a groove along the length of the line.

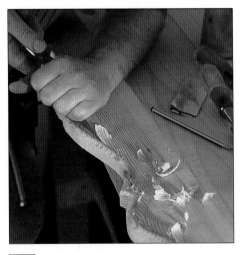

7 Set in the background along the line with a chisel. This line can be up to about ¼ inch (4 mm) in depth and is for decorative purposes. When you have completed the chiseling, sand to a smooth finish.

8 Damage all of the pieces heavily using the broken surface of a brick, a set of keys, or some other sharp object (see page 96). Sand all of the dents back to a rough finish with coarse sandpaper.

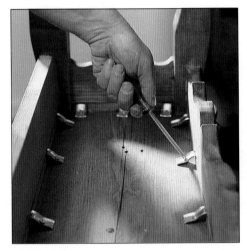

9 Assemble sides and legs, glue ends of dowels and clamp. Glue rails in place. Stain base and table-top. When dry, fit table-top to rails with clips. Finish with a thin coat of varnish and apply bees' wax.

LEG CUTTING DETAIL

STEP 1: Using a leg profile template (see page 156) draw the leg profile on to the top and underside of the square section of timber. Flip the template over and draw the profile on to the front and back of the timber (as shown here by a dotted line). Cut the first pattern using a bandsaw or large jigsaw. These are labeled on the diagram as the first and second cuts.

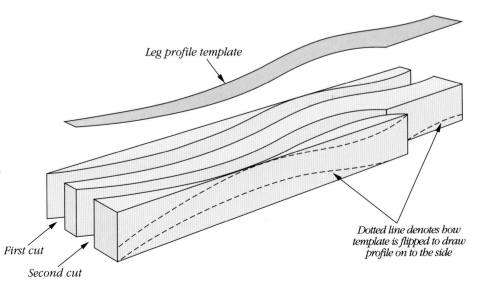

Leg profile template

First cut

Second cut

Dotted line denotes how template is flipped to draw profile on to the side

DETAILED VIEW

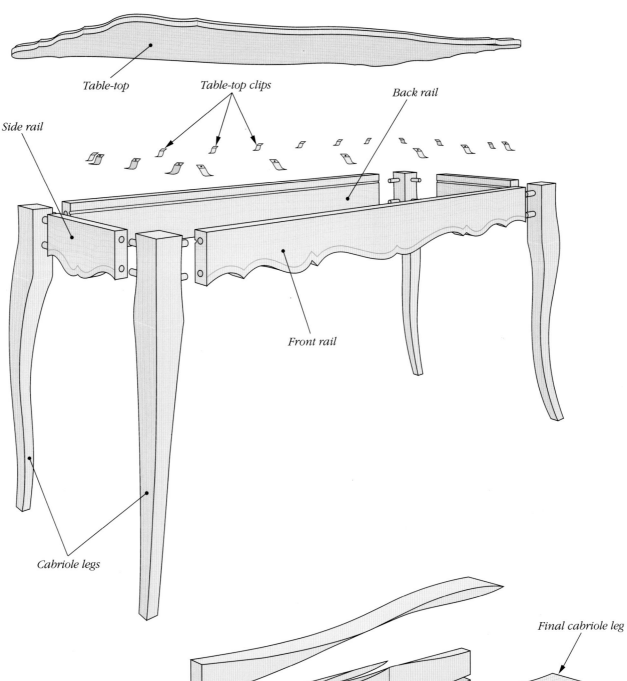

Table-top

Table-top clips

Back rail

Side rail

Front rail

Cabriole legs

Final cabriole leg

Third cut

Fourth cut

Third cut

Fourth cut

STEP 2: Re-bundle the offcuts and tape them together to re-form the original block of wood. This is done to create an easy shape for working with. Make the third and fourth cuts to create the final shape of the cabriole leg.

TREEN OF THE BRITISH ISLES

Before the use of materials such as pottery, ceramics, pewter, glass and plastics, small everyday objects like spoons, platters, goblets and boxes were made from wood. These small, carefully crafted objects, usually made from a single piece of wood, are known as Treen or Treenware.

Butter pats

There are many suggestions as to the origin of the term Treen. Some accounts say it is the Old English plural for tree, just as "shoen" was the plural of shoe; others suggest that its origins include a reference to the technique of "turning" wood on a lathe to create the objects, and in this sense the term has been used to describe small pottery pieces turned on the potter's wheel. Whatever its origins, today the term Treen is used to describe wooden household items no larger than a spinning wheel.

Wood was readily available throughout the British Isles and required little preparation, other than drying, before it could be used for making utensils. Once made, the objects did not need firing or other complex finishing before they could be used. Treenware is still prized for the qualities the original owners valued: the beauty and variety of the wood's grain and its natural hues and colors; smoothness to the touch; a simple elegance of form and a lustrous patina which develops with use over time.

Treen objects are usually made in one piece and seldom have any extra pieces attached by gluing or joining. They were passed down with pride from generation to generation, many wills from past centuries contained specific instructions to ensure the fair distribution of the family "Treenware."

The timbers were selected for the properties which were required in the finished object, *Pastry cutter* generally hardwoods were favored over softwoods. Lignum vitae, the hardest of all woods, was a highly prized material. It is an extremely dense and heavy wood because it retains most of its natural oils and was suitable for use only by more experienced craftspeople, whose skill, strength and patience resulted in works revealing the natural beauty of the dark grain, which is streaked with yellow or green.

A marvelous selection of Treenware gives this dresser a delightfully rustic style.

The elegant simplicity of this bowl is characteristic of the Treen style.

DESIGNS AND VARIATIONS

A wide variety of Treen objects were made, and many fine examples are still sold and collected throughout the world. Treenware was made by whatever combination of carving and turning was appropriate for the piece. A mouse trap was made with sealed sliding doors which were operated by a series of weights and pulleys. Treenware for the meal table included cutting boards, bowls, goblets, salt and pepper pots, trays, and Wassail bowls with covers and dipper cups.

CANDLE HOLDERS
Many varieties of household objects were made from wood, such as candle holders, board games and bowling pins; inkstands, and quill holders.

BUTTER MOLD
Utensils for food had to be made from wood which was flavorless, and could be repeatedly washed and used without splitting, cracking or warping.

SALT BOX
Kitchen Treenware included, salt boxes, stackable spice pots, rolling pins, mortar and pestle, tea caddies, grinders, lemon squeezers, buckets and funnels.

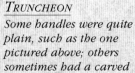

TRUNCHEON
Some handles were quite plain, such as the one pictured above; others sometimes had a carved hand for a handle.

LOVE SPOONS
Some pieces involved elaborate decorative carving, especially items which were created as "tokens" such as these Welsh love spoons.

TRINKET BOX
This box is made from walnut burl which grows on the tree trunk and, when cut, reveals a colorful and varied grain. Burls are in great demand for making ornamental objects.

TIMBERS
Woods such as sycamore, fruitwood, cherry, maple and mahogany were all very popular.

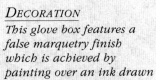

DECORATION
This glove box features a false marquetry finish which is achieved by painting over an ink drawn design on the light wood.

Cherry

Rose mahogany

English walnut

Rose maple

PROJECT: TREEN CANDLEHOLDER

This simple and elegant Treen candleholder is put together using only glue, which makes it an ideal project for the beginning woodworker. The side pieces protect the candle flame from drafts and the hole allows the finished product to be mounted on a wall.

Level of difficulty: Beginner

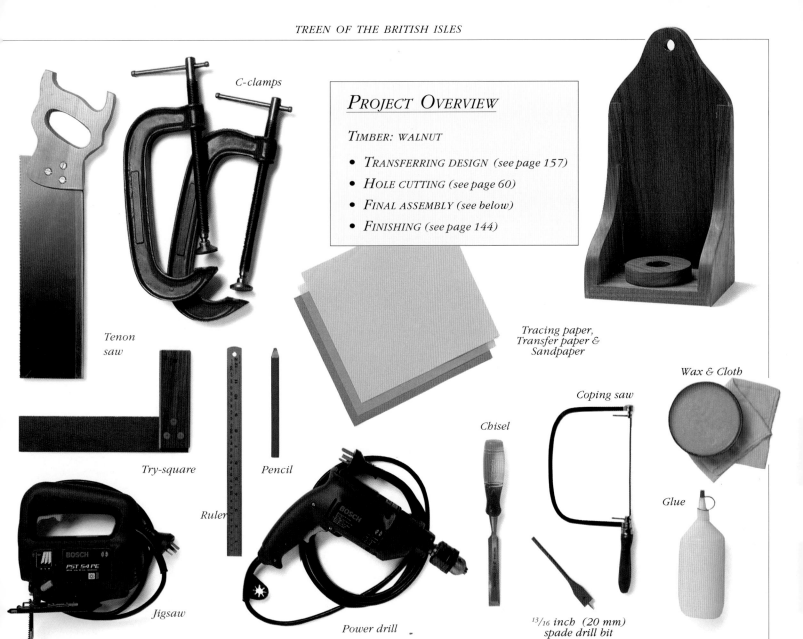

C-clamps

Tenon saw

PROJECT OVERVIEW

TIMBER: WALNUT

- *TRANSFERRING DESIGN* (see page 157)
- *HOLE CUTTING* (see page 60)
- *FINAL ASSEMBLY* (see below)
- *FINISHING* (see page 144)

Tracing paper, Transfer paper & Sandpaper

Wax & Cloth

Try-square

Pencil

Ruler

Chisel

Coping saw

Glue

Jigsaw

Power drill

¹³/₁₆ inch (20 mm) spade drill bit

WOODWORK STEP-BY-STEP

1 Cut the timber to size. Transfer the pattern onto the timber. Mark the designs to be cut, using a pencil (or sharp knife), compass and a ruler as needed.

2 Drill a ³/₈ inch (8 mm) hole in the back piece, to hang the candleholder on the wall. Using a spade bit, drill a ¹³/₁₆ inch (20 mm) hole in center of doughnutpiece.

3 Clamp the timber in place to cut. Cut out pieces for the candleholder sides, the back and the base from the timber, using the jigsaw (see page 139).

4 Using the tenon saw and a chisel (see page 139), cut a $1/2$ x $1/4$ inch (12 x 6 mm) rabbet along the base of each of the side pieces. This is to slot the base piece into.

5 Sand all of the pieces. Assemble the pieces and glue them all into their positions. Lightly clamp all of the pieces together until they are completely dry.

6 Cut around the outside of doughnut piece with the coping saw. Sand the edges and glue doughnut in position on the base of candleholder. Wax to finish.

HOLE CUTTING

The center holes for the doughnut and the back of the candleholder should be cut out from the pattern on the large piece of wood, before the pieces themselves are cut away from the timber. This gives you more surface to work with and makes the job of cutting the holes significantly easier. Once the pattern has been transferred to the wood, use a spade drill bit to cut out the holes. Use a jigsaw to cut the other pieces from the timber and finally use a coping saw to cut around the outside of the doughnut.

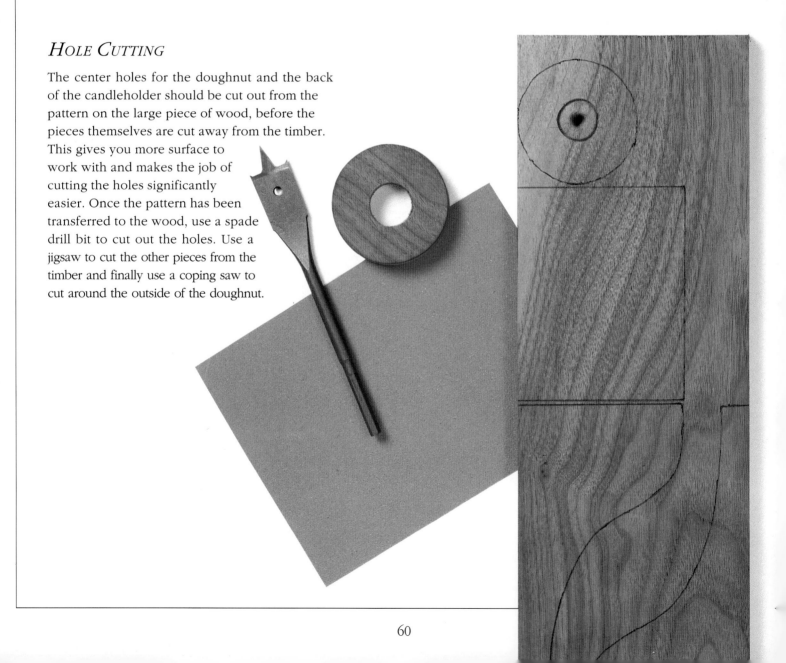

DETAILED VIEW

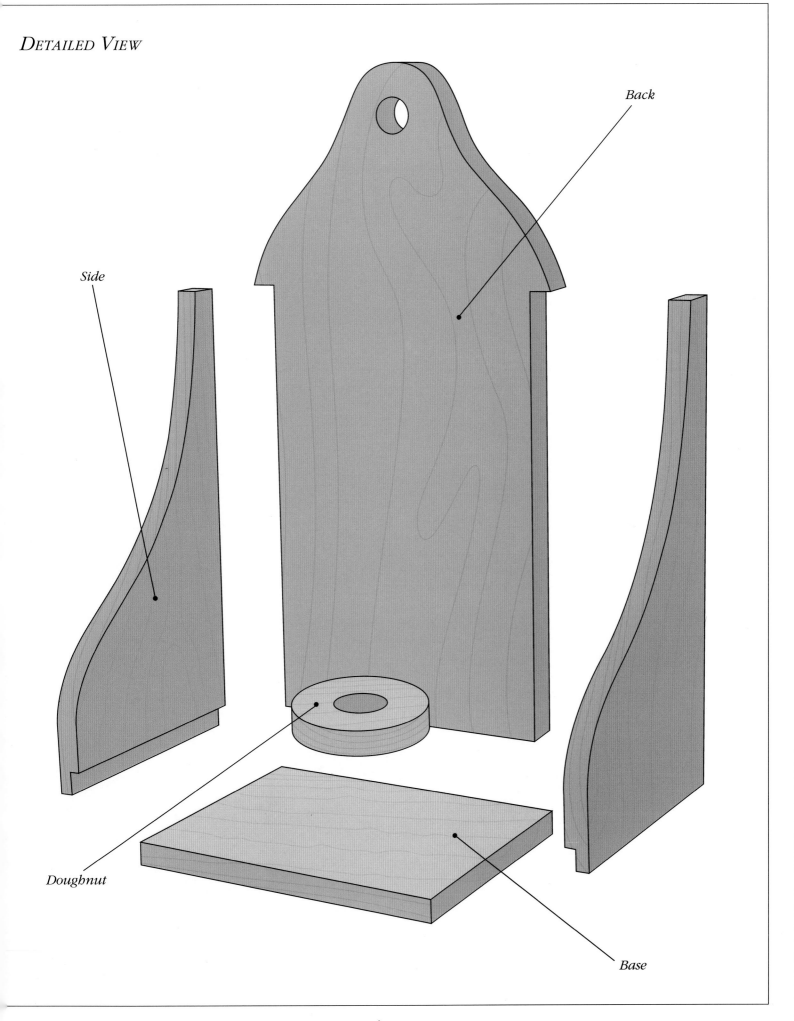

Side

Back

Doughnut

Base

PROJECT: TREEN TRINKET BOX

Most Treen objects are made from a single piece of timber, but this project includes a second type of timber to enhance an otherwise plain box. An inlay of English walnut adds elegance to the finished product. Accuracy is important for a neat fit.

Level of difficulty: Intermediate

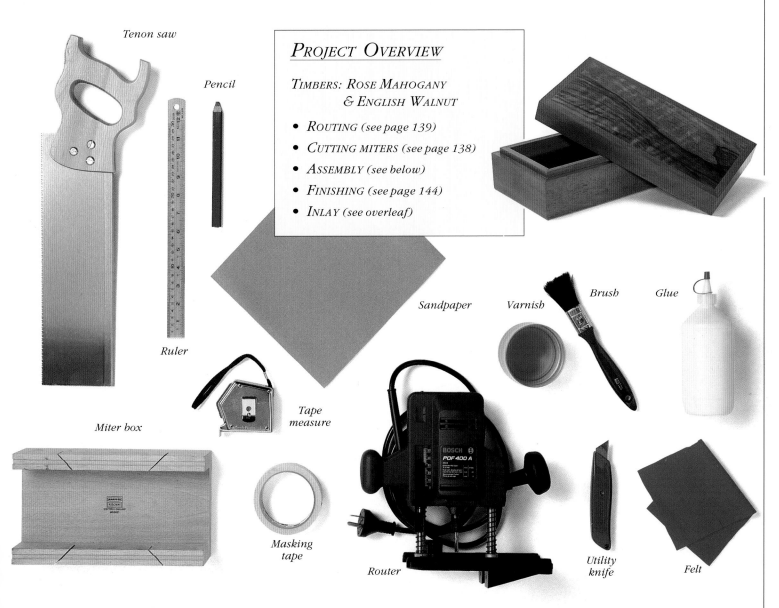

Tenon saw

Pencil

PROJECT OVERVIEW

TIMBERS: ROSE MAHOGANY
& ENGLISH WALNUT

- ROUTING (see page 139)
- CUTTING MITERS (see page 138)
- ASSEMBLY (see below)
- FINISHING (see page 144)
- INLAY (see overleaf)

Ruler

Sandpaper

Varnish

Brush

Glue

Miter box

Tape measure

Masking tape

Router

Utility knife

Felt

WOODWORKING STEP-BY-STEP

1 Cut timber to the required widths (see page 158). Rout a ¼ inch (6 mm) rabbet along both edges of the box and the lid pieces then cut all of the timber to length.

2 Tape the lid and the box lengths together. Using the miter box, cut miters at 45° to give two 7¹/₁₆ inch (180 mm) side sections and two 3⁹/₁₆ inch (90 mm) end sections.

3 Glue the box frame and lid frame separately, checking for a neat fit. Hold each frame in place with masking tape until the glue is completely dry.

4 Cut the walnut top piece $^1/_{16}$ inch (1 mm) larger than the lid rabbet and then file and sand down for a perfect fit (see page 140). Glue the top into the lid rabbet.

5 Cut the plywood base to fit the box rabbet. If necessary, stain plywood a suitable color. Glue a piece of felt to the less attractive side of the plywood and trim it to size.

6 Lacquer the box with clear varnish and allow to dry in a dust-free environment. When dry, glue the base into the box rabbet, so the felt is inside the box.

INLAY

In true inlay work, or intarsia, pieces of wood are inserted into prepared recesses in a contrasting wood. This technique was developed in Italy and spread to France, Germany and Holland where it was a popular means of decorating furniture. This project takes a simpler approach, with the piece of walnut placed in a recessed frame, which still produces a very good effect.

Detailed View

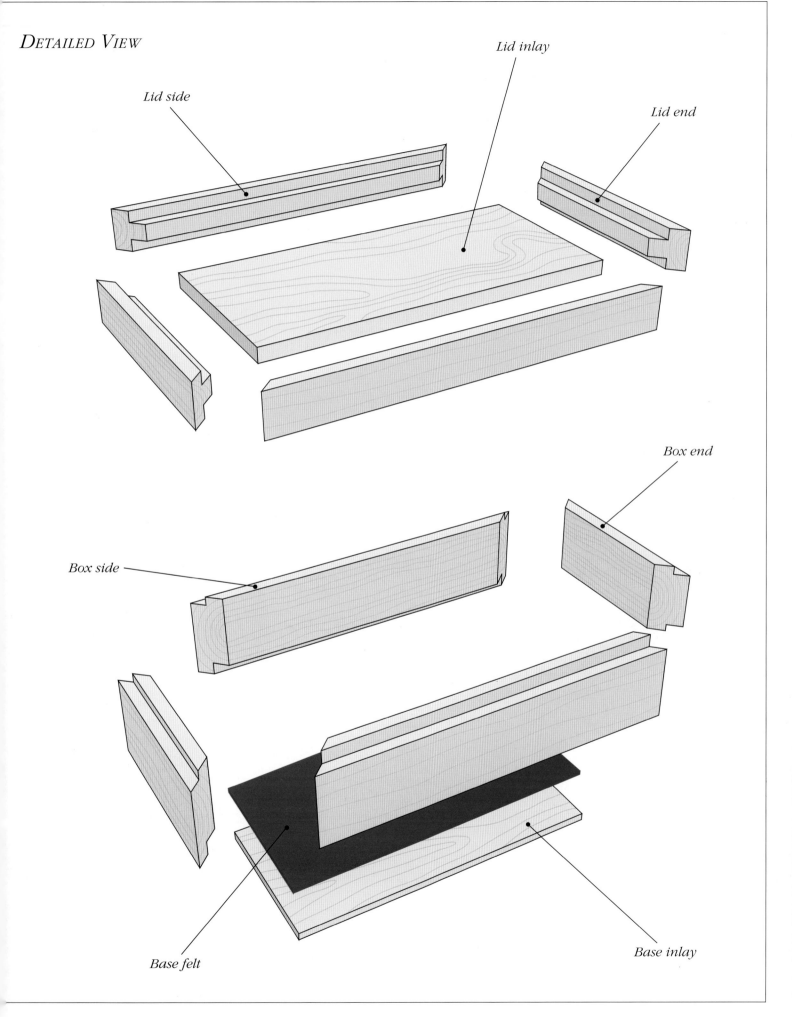

Lid side

Lid inlay

Lid end

Box end

Box side

Base felt

Base inlay

GERMAN TRADITION

The history of German furniture design has been greatly affected by numerous European trends in art and architecture: Romanesque, Gothic, Renaissance, baroque and rococo. During these periods, the most interesting pieces of German woodcraft came from peasant folk living in the alpine regions. With the rise of classicism, the unaffected designs and sturdy forms of German furniture makers came into their own.

Wine barrel

During the Middle Ages heavy basic furniture was often built into the construction of a house. Apart from tables and chairs, one of the first 'mobile' pieces (the word *moebel* is German for furniture) was the storage chest. It was generally made from pine, ash or oak and the surface was treated with hot wax. Its construction, however, changed as different techniques of preparing and joining wood were developed. Before the growth of sawmills in the fifteenth century, boards were split from a tree trunk and hewn flat. These coarse pieces were fitted together by carpenters using mortise and tenon joints.

When sawn boards became available, skilled joiners butt-joined pieces to form chests similar to the project featured in this chapter. Eventually, the fashion developed for frame-and-panel constructions using tongue in groove joints.

A chest was an almost essential item in a bride's dowry. It was sometimes accompanied by other pieces—a bed, an armoire, a side-board, and a corner cupboard—all were decorated to match one another. Early German pieces were stenciled in one or two colors, or else decorated with some simple chip carving. The designs chosen were geometrical such as stars, diamonds or sun wheels and many of them symbolized earlier pagan beliefs. A demand for skilled artists and carvers grew, and such artisans went on to create more elaborate paintings and relief carvings, with hearts, flowers and birds featuring among the most popular motifs.

Bedside cabinet

In the latter half of the eighteenth century, a classical style evolved and German woodworkers gained a lasting reputation for simple and functional designs made with great attention to construction and detail.

Richly grained woods combine with classic German styles in this charming rural inn.

Bavarian cuckoo clock

DESIGNS AND VARIATIONS

Germany's tradition of decorative carving is today alive and thriving, particularly in Bavaria. The state runs carving schools in the village of Oberammergau, where master carvers pass on their unsurpassed skill at carving religious figures, scenes, cuckoo clocks and decorative items. The wood carvers of Oberammergau are world famous for their Passion Play. Painted floral designs and rural settings are popular forms of decoration for wooden pieces.

PAINTED DECORATION
Decoration was inspired by the symmetry and richness of flowers, as shown on this writing desk.

STYLES
A variety of simple chair styles are characteristic of German furniture. These often served as milking stools too.

CHAIRS
Religious and pagan symbols such as hearts, geometric designs and stylized human figures are featured on these various chair backs.

WARDROBE
Frame-and-panel construction meant that large pieces such as this wardrobe were sturdy and durable but comparatively lightweight.

NOAH'S ARK
Pairs of animals are stored inside this simple wooden ark, which consists of a house resting on a flat-bottomed barge.

CROCKERY RACK
This elegantly carved rack features some of the more popular motifs in German decorative style, such as hearts and stars.

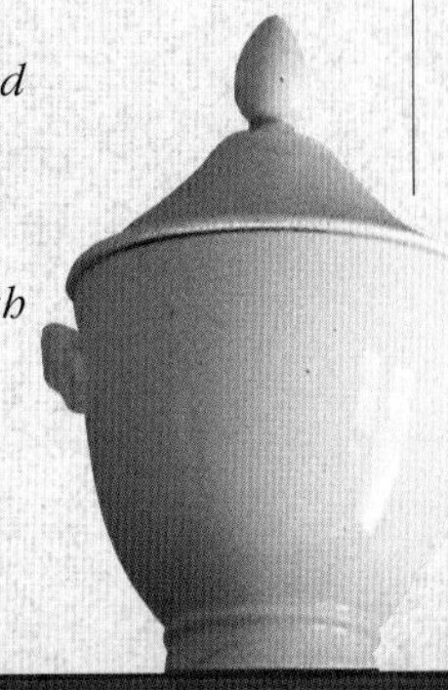

SPANSCHACHTEL
Intarsia was often imitated through the use of clever painting techniques, as shown on the lid of this dowry box.

TIMBERS
Pine, ash and oak were generally used for furniture making and were treated with hot wax.

Oak

Walnut

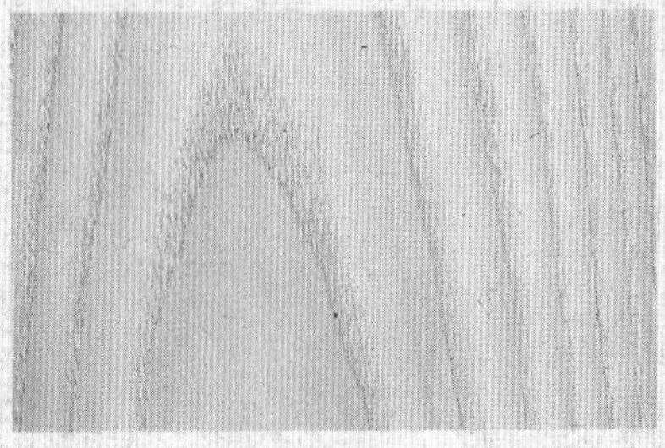

Ash

PROJECT: BAVARIAN BLANKET CHEST

The making and decoration of a blanket chest was an important part of the
Bavarian wedding ritual, a tradition which accompanied German immigrants
to America. This doweled chest has been painted with a charming design
of flowers and a heart which are both traditional Bauernmalerei motifs.

Level of difficulty: Advanced

24 inch
(600 mm)
C-clamps

Bar clamp

Tracing paper,
Transfer paper
& Sandpaper

Ruler

PROJECT OVERVIEW

TIMBER: RADIATA PINE

- LAMINATING (see page 18)
- TRANSFERRING DESIGN (see page 159)
- JIGSAWING (see page 141)
- DOWELS (see page 72)
- FITTING CLEATS & LID (see below)
- HINGING (see page 72)
- ASSEMBLY (see below)
- FINISHING (see page 144)

Wax & Cloth

Router

Dowels   Stain

Glue

Pencil

Chisels

4d (40 mm)
finish nails

#5 x 1 inch flat
head wood
screws

Tape
measure

Hand
panel saw

Screw-
driver

Hand plane   Jigsaw   Power drill   Carpenter's
mallet

6 foot
(1800 mm)
piano hinge

Claw hammer

WOODWORKING STEP-BY-STEP

1 Cut pieces to width (see page 159). Plane all edges square. Laminate panel pieces and clamp together, lay flat and support with extra blocks. Plane all faces to remove excess glue, cut to length.

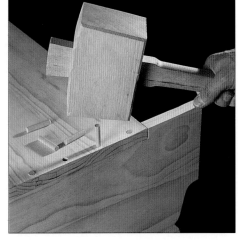

2 Cut the side patterns with a jigsaw. Plane and sand inside and clamp. Assemble the box sides. Drill ³/₈ inch (8 mm) holes along the edges as indicated. Coat the dowels with glue and hammer into place.

3 Fit the cleats inside the box, glue and clamp until dry. Cleats can be tacked after gluing for additional strength. Place the base pieces in position under the box and nail in position to secure.

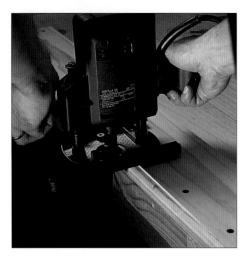

4 Fit the lid and clamp in position then drill. Use a router to rout a molding around the outside edges of the lid; this is for decorative purposes only.

5 Chamfer both sections of the lid (see page 141) to house the piano hinge and then fix the hinge in place by using 1 inch (20 mm) flat head wood screws.

6 Dowel the lid in place. Plane and sand. If you would prefer, you can stain and/or paint the chest with a simple design of your choice to complete.

USING DOWELS

Dowels for joints can be bought ready made or you can cut and shape your own. Cut thin dowel to length and chamfer one end with a knife. Drill a pilot hole with the appropriate bit. Coat the dowel with glue and insert it into the pilot hole, chamfered end first. Tap it in with a mallet and sand off any projection. See page 143 for more detail.

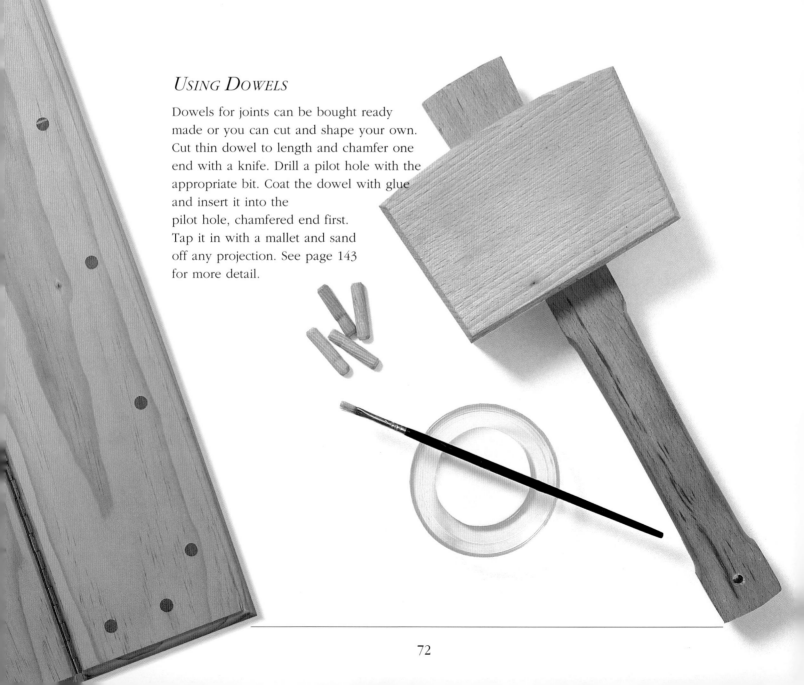

DETAILED VIEW

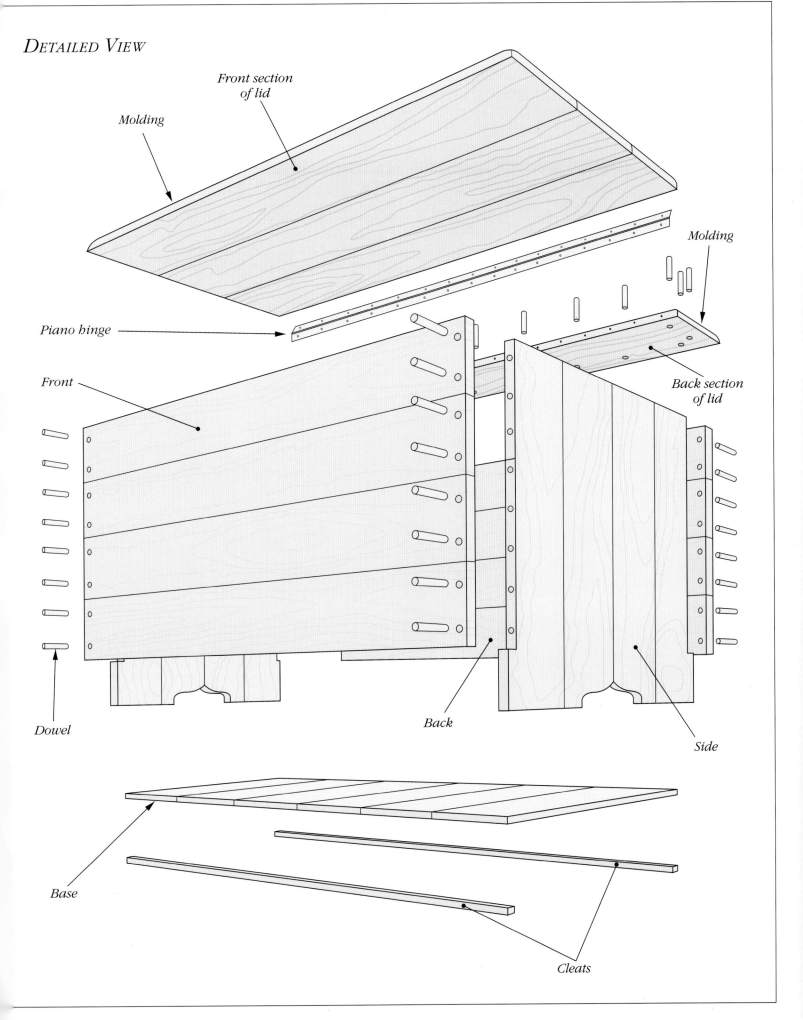

Front section
of lid

Molding

Molding

Piano hinge

Back section
of lid

Front

Dowel

Back

Side

Base

Cleats

Project: German Candle Box

When candles were the main source of lighting for the home, keeping them safe from mice was essential. The plain lines of this candle box are softened by the carving of a tulip motif and the application of a delicately colored wash.

Level of difficulty: Beginner

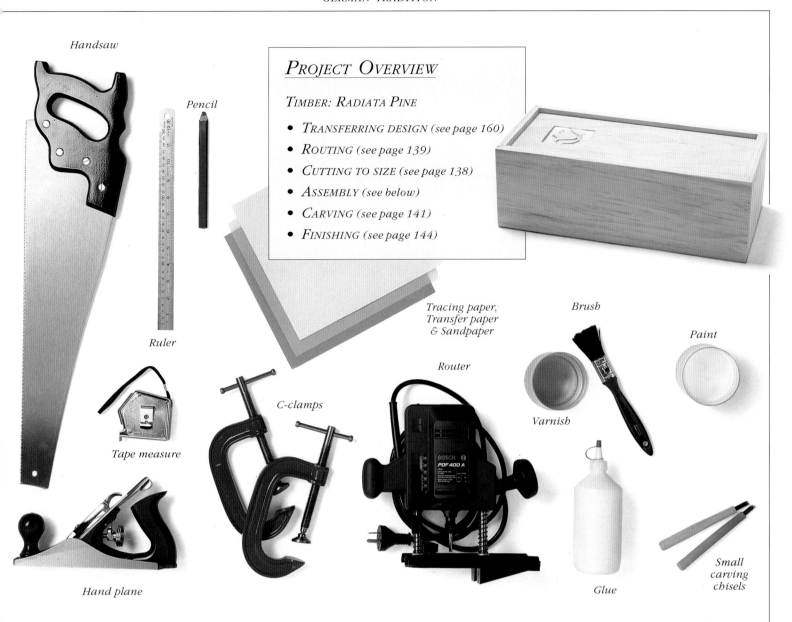

Handsaw

Pencil

PROJECT OVERVIEW

TIMBER: RADIATA PINE

- *TRANSFERRING DESIGN (see page 160)*
- *ROUTING (see page 139)*
- *CUTTING TO SIZE (see page 138)*
- *ASSEMBLY (see below)*
- *CARVING (see page 141)*
- *FINISHING (see page 144)*

Ruler

Tracing paper,
Transfer paper
& Sandpaper

Brush

Paint

Router

Varnish

Tape measure

C-clamps

Hand plane

Glue

Small
carving
chisels

WOODWORKING STEP-BY-STEP

1 Cut all the pieces as indicated (see page 160). Take the piece for the sides and square off one of the edges. Rout the bottom groove ¼ x ¼ inch (6 x 6 mm) deep.

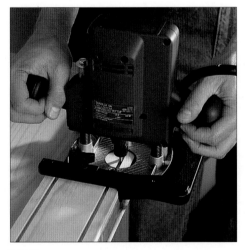

2 Rout the top groove on the side length, ¼ x ¼ inch (6 x 6 mm) deep. Cut sides to length using miter box and tenon saw. Trim narrow end piece to correct size.

3 Rout the rabbets on the ends of all sides. Clamp and rout a ¼ x ⁵⁄₁₆ inch (6 x 7 mm) rabbet around all edges of the lid and base piece. Cut lid and base timber to length.

4 Sand the inside of the box to a very smooth finish. Assemble the sides and base. Glue the pieces and clamp them together very lightly until the glue is dry.

5 Transfer the tulip motif (see page 160) on to the lid, using the pencil, transfer paper and tracing paper. You can use a design of your own if you prefer.

6 Outline the pencil drawn motif on the lid with a straight cutting tool, then cut at a slight angle away from the center of the shape to a depth of about 1/8 inch (2-3 mm).

7 Carve out the background using a U-shaped gouge (see page 141), so that it is of a uniform depth. Sand the carved background area lightly.

8 Glue the handle on to the lid. Sand outside surfaces. Thin some acrylic paint with water and paint a light wash over all surfaces. Varnish to complete.

Tools for cutting linoleum are suitable for cutting this design in a soft timber. You will need a straight blade and a U-shaped cutter.

DETAILED VIEW

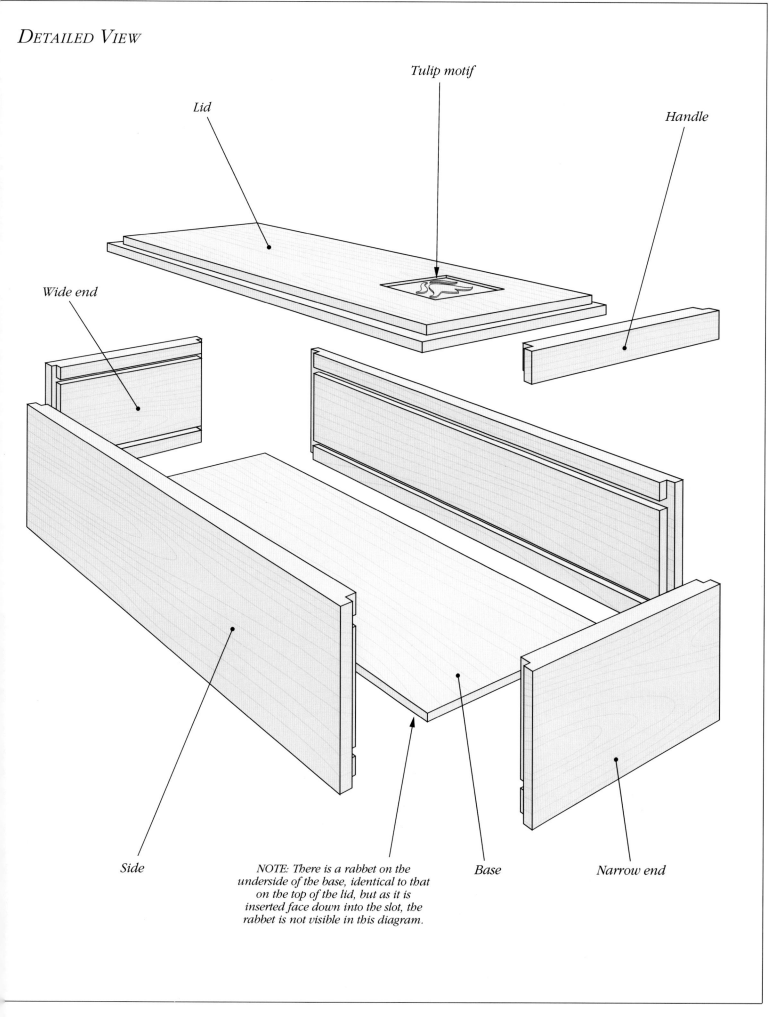

Tulip motif

Lid

Handle

Wide end

Side

NOTE: There is a rabbet on the underside of the base, identical to that on the top of the lid, but as it is inserted face down into the slot, the rabbet is not visible in this diagram.

Base

Narrow end

RUSSIAN TOYS

WHAT BETTER OCCUPATION to while away the long, severely cold nights of Russian winters than the making of wooden toys? Restless adults were kept occupied in front of the fire. The pile of firewood ensured a steady material supply, and the fire offered an easy way to dispose of the chips and scraps produced. The wooden toys then kept the children amused throughout the seemingly countless days of winter.

Pull-string bear

Russia has probably the most easily identifiable "national" toy, that is the *Matryushka* nesting dolls. The origins of these dolls is unclear, although their existence has been well documented since the early 19th century. One suggestion is that they are a very imaginative solution to the age old problem of explaining the impending arrival of a new baby brother or sister to existing children! The sets usually consist of seven precisely sized dolls. Each of the first six opens to reveal another doll concealed inside.

All the dolls are brightly decorated. The last, smallest doll is always a solid piece which does not open. Sometimes the largest doll contains a set of bowling pins and a small ball, or a set of small tumbler dolls.

Variations in the patterns used for decoration include painting some of the dolls carrying the traditional welcoming gifts of bread and salt, or game such as a rabbit or goose. The hollow dolls offer great hiding places for many children's treasures. A popular game involves guessing which doll conceals a sweet or some other treasure. The correct guess wins the hidden prize.

Matryushka dolls are now made in a variety of shapes, sizes and characters.

A lesser-known wooden Russian doll is the *Trihedral* which is carved from a single, triangular piece of wood on a base block which allows it to stand upright. The doll's features and clothes are carved into the design and then painted for emphasis. *Trihedral* dolls are made in many varieties, from peasant families, to nobility and soldiers.

Russia is also renowned for its moving toys, including pecking hens, balanced toys, moving scenes and weighted tumbler dolls. Tumbler dolls conceal a heavy weight in their base which keeps them rocking back up to a standing position when they are pushed down. Pecking birds or chicks make use of a leverage or pendulum system to rock a wooden bird back and forth on its base to simulate pecking at a little food or water dish.

Razvod is Russian for "moving apart" and describes carved scenes created on a jointed trellis. The scenes are animated by the trellis being manipulated like a pair of scissors, so that the carved figures move towards and away from the central point of the design.

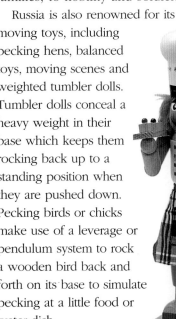

Nutcracker doll

DESIGNS AND VARIATIONS

Russia contains some of the largest forest resources in the world. It spans across desert, tundra, forest, and sub-tropical areas and produces a fabulous variety of forests including both deciduous and evergreen trees, although hardwood timbers are relatively scarce. With such an abundance of natural materials available, it is not surprising that a tradition of intricate and clever wooden toys has developed. Many Russian wooden toys were decorated in the brilliant reds and yellows glorified by followers of the sun cult.

NESTED EGGS
Matryushka *dolls are also sometimes made in different shapes, such as the egg pictured here.*

SWADDLING DOLL
The swaddling doll became popular in Russia in the 19th century.

MATRYUSHKA DOLLS
A set of these famous dolls is reputed to have been used to smuggle NATO secrets from Paris to Russia in 1966.

TIMBERS
Russia's abundant forests produce birch, fir, larch, maple, elm, oak, pine, cedar, linden and spruce among others.

Aspen

FOLK TOYS
The bear with honey pot and boy with balalaika are carved and decorated with charming naiveté.

Willow

ROCKING DOLL
Toys which can be manipulated are a Russian specialty. This baby is rocked by means of a string which is threaded through the center of the doll.

Beech

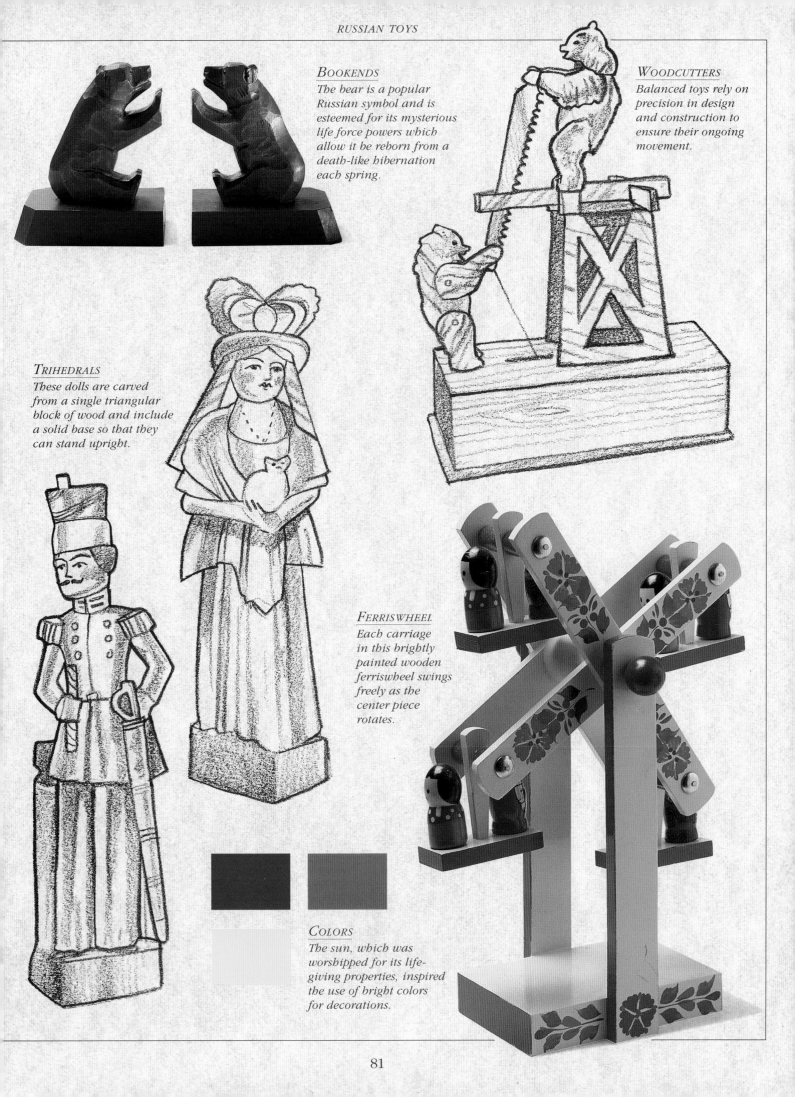

BOOKENDS
The bear is a popular Russian symbol and is esteemed for its mysterious life force powers which allow it be reborn from a death-like hibernation each spring.

WOODCUTTERS
Balanced toys rely on precision in design and construction to ensure their ongoing movement.

TRIHEDRALS
These dolls are carved from a single triangular block of wood and include a solid base so that they can stand upright.

FERRISWHEEL
Each carriage in this brightly painted wooden ferriswheel swings freely as the center piece rotates.

COLORS
The sun, which was worshipped for its life-giving properties, inspired the use of bright colors for decorations.

PROJECT: RUSSIAN WOODCUTTERS

By alternately pushing and pulling the base rods of this very simple toy, you coax a peasant and a bear to cooperate wonderfully to chop wood. One variation on the piece features a blacksmithing pair, who take turns striking an anvil with their mallets.

Level of difficulty: Beginner

Ruler

Pencil

C-clamps

PROJECT OVERVIEW

TIMBER: MAPLE

- PROFILING (see page 138)
- FILING (see page 140)
- ASSEMBLY (see below)
- FINISHING (see page 144)

Tracing paper,
Transfer paper
& Sandpaper

Varnish

Brush

Tack
hammer

Paint

Tape measure

2 x ⅝ inch
tacks

Hand
drill

Coping
saw

4 x #6 x ¾ inch
wood
screws

Tenon
saw

Glue

File

Screwdriver

WOODWORKING STEP-BY-STEP

1 Transfer the patterns (see page 161) and cut out the two figures and the chopping block using the coping saw (see page 138). File and sand the edges, taking special care to round off any sharp corners.

2 With a tenon saw, cut the rod into two pieces, each 12⅝ inches (320 mm) long. Sand them smooth and round the ends. Mark screw positions as shown, drill holes and assemble with brass round head screws.

3 Attach the chopping block to the base with glue and fix it with two tacks. Paint the toy, including any facial expressions and clothes as required. Then distress and varnish to complete the toy.

PROJECT: RUSSIAN PECKING HENS

In this ingenious moving toy, a swinging weight causes the hens to peck at the platter in sequence. The trick is in getting the balance just right: you will need to test the action carefully before finally tying the weight to the string which is threaded through the platter.

Level of difficulty: Beginner

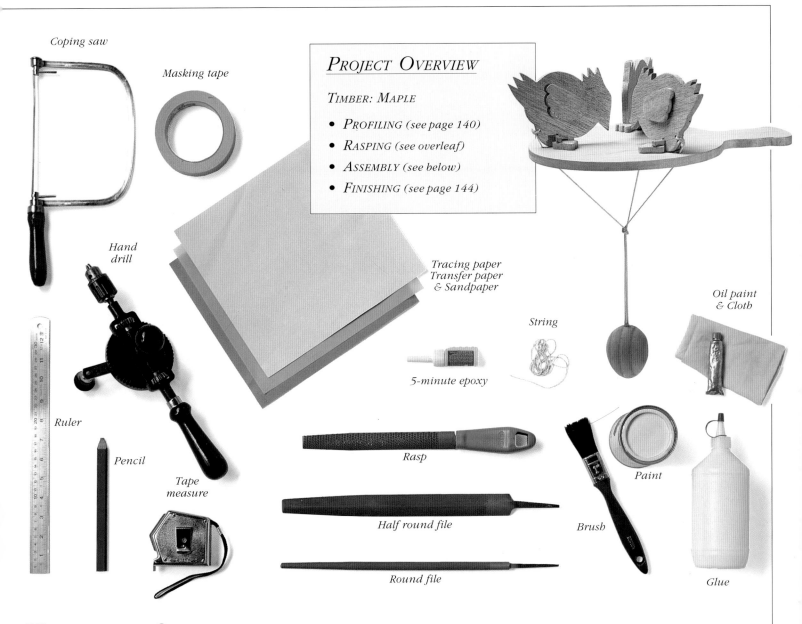

Coping saw

Masking tape

PROJECT OVERVIEW

TIMBER: MAPLE

- PROFILING (see page 140)
- RASPING (see overleaf)
- ASSEMBLY (see below)
- FINISHING (see page 144)

Hand drill

Tracing paper
Transfer paper
& Sandpaper

Oil paint
& Cloth

String

Ruler

5-minute epoxy

Pencil

Rasp

Paint

Tape measure

Half round file

Brush

Round file

Glue

WOODWORKING STEP-BY-STEP

1 Transfer the patterns (page 162) and cut shapes with a coping saw. Holding pieces in a vice, file and sand the edges, rounding all of the corners slightly. Cut the dowel into three pieces, each 1³/₁₆ inches (30 mm) long.

2 Drill three large holes and three small holes through the hens as indicated. Tie a 9¹/₁₆ inch (230 mm) string through the small hole. Glue the wings on to the hens. Drill three holes through the platter.

3 Glue the feet in pairs on the platter, ensuring they are evenly spaced around the platter and the same distance from the edge. Place each hen between a pair of feet and glue the dowels to the feet.

4 Thread the string from each of the hens through the nearest hole in the platter. Gather even lengths of the three strings, draw them together at the center beneath the platter, and tie a firm knot.

5 Rasp a small block of wood into an egg shape and sand it until smooth. Alternatively, purchase a wooden egg or large wooden bead. Drill a small hole in the base of the wider end of the egg.

6 Thread the three strings into the hole at the base of the egg and glue in position with a strong, fast drying glue. Secure with a small wooden wedge. Paint and antique to complete (see below).

ANTIQUING

The newly painted hens have been given a patina of age through the process of antiquing. Concentrate on areas which would be most worn, such as the handle, and on cracks where grime would collect. An antiquing patina is applied with a soft cloth, then oil paint is brushed on and blended in as required.

Detailed View

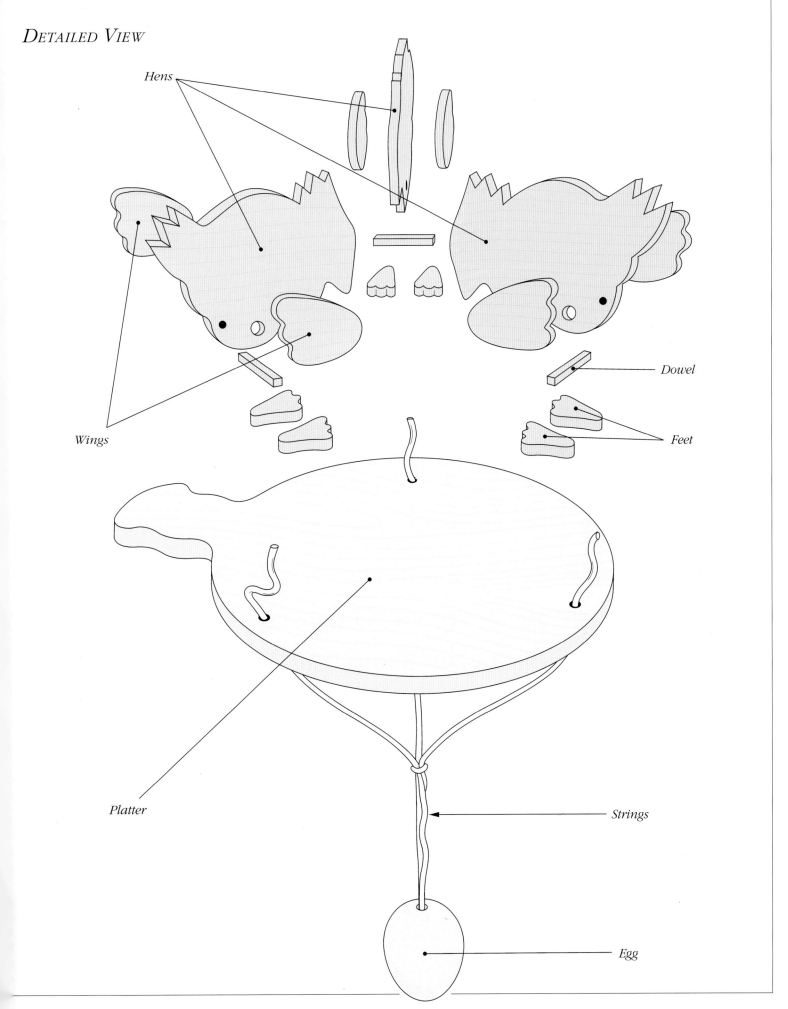

Hens

Wings

Dowel

Feet

Platter

Strings

Egg

MEXICAN WOODCRAFT

THE COMBINATION OF PRE-CHRISTIAN and Christian influences on the culture is clearly visible in the designs and decorations of Mexico. The beauty and variety of nature is recreated and embellished, along with other, more fanciful images that emerge from ancient spiritual depths.

Maracas

Mexico's geography spans from tropical rainforests, through to temperate areas, and consequently, it provides an enormous range of natural materials for local woodworkers to choose from. Woodcrafts form a central part of everyday life; many objects are made and decorated for use and ornamentation in the home as well as for traditional festivals.

Wooden puppets, dolls, yo-yos, tops, animal-shaped money boxes, and ornaments delight both adults and children alike, Castanets, maracas made from gourds, and many other instruments are crafted and decorated in the characteristically vivid Mexican style. Wood is also used for a variety of functional objects, from very large pieces of furniture down to small household goods such as trays and baskets.

Nature inspires many of the motifs for decoration: animals, plants, flowers, the sun, moon and stars are frequently depicted. Humorous portrayals of skeletons are also popular. Bright colors and attractive patterns are more highly prized than realistic images.

Nature is also put to good use in finishing woodwork pieces: local adult tree-parasites are boiled, crushed and sieved to create *aje* for fixing powders; cats' hair is used for making the bristles in home-made paint brushes; and the finished objects are often buried in the ant hills to give them an aged appearance.

Picture frame

Mexico has a very long-standing tradition of using lacquer finishes on wooden objects. In Uruapan, the elaborate task of *embutido*, or encrustation, requires several stages. The finished piece is lacquered in a single color, using *aje,* then the design is excised with a sharp instrument and the hollows are filled in with different colored lacquers, then the lighter shades of lacquer are inlaid last.

These elaborately carved wooden whisks are used for beating milk shakes and other dairy products.

Great skill and care is put into the decorative carving of objects.

DESIGNS AND VARIATIONS

Spain dominated many parts of the world from the early sixteenth century, including areas as diverse as Mexico and the Philippines. Mexican culture and crafts absorbed the new and exotic images of Spanish Catholicism and South East Asian vibrancy and retained their own strong and lively traditions. The result is a joyous naiveté of style which is characteristic of Mexican woodcraft.

ANIMALS
Brightly colored animals, both domestic and wild, are often used in the decoration of wooden pieces. A lively appearance is more important than a life-like one.

FURNITURE
The decorative hole at the top of the mirror doubles as a way to hang this dresser on the wall.

BASKET
Many pieces, like this basket, are left undecorated, but the wood may be finished by waxing or varnishing.

Mahogany

Blackwood

TIMBERS
Mexican wood-workers can choose from a variety of timbers, such as copal, pine, oak, cedar and primavera.

Balsa

MASKS
Mask makers from Guerrero are particularly famous for their vividly painted, carved wooden masks.

LACQUERWARE
Profuse, brightly colored decorations are frequently finished off with the skillful application of numerous coats of lacquer, as shown on this trinket box.

CARVING
The elaborate carving on this chair shows the influence of the early sun-worshipping cultures of Mexico.

AZTEC PATTERNS
Many decorative patterns continue the traditions of the Aztecs, who worked extensively with repetitive geometric shapes.

91

PROJECT: MEXICAN FRAME

In Mexico, the craftsperson makes use of whatever materials or
ideas comes to hand. In the same spirit, this project takes old
moldings and skirting boards and, using only basic techniques
and tools, transforms them into an eye-catching frame.

Level of difficulty: Beginner

PROJECT OVERVIEW

TIMBER: VARIOUS

- *CUTTING MITERS (see page 138)*
- *ROUTING (see page 139)*
- *ASSEMBLY (see below)*
- *FINISHING (see page 144)*

Tenon saw

Handsaw

Sandpaper

Ruler

Pencil

Brush

Paint stripper

Picture-hanging wire

Tape measure

Try-square

Sliding bevel

Screws & Eyelets

Miter box

Glue

Screwdriver

WOODWORKING STEP-BY-STEP

1 Select old timber and strip off the paint. Arrange in layers with the widest piece as a base. Mark and cut 45° miters on the ends of each piece.

2 Chisel a rabbet along the back of the base pieces. Make sure it is deep enough and wide enough to hold whatever piece of artwork you plan to frame.

3 Glue the layers together to create four separate sides and then glue the mitered edges together. On the back, screw eyelets and thread wire for hanging.

PROJECT: MEXICAN SUN PLAQUE

The rooms of a Mexican home are sometimes sparsely furnished but seldom unadorned: frames, small altars and crucifixes often fill the walls. In this project, a roughly carved sun which hints at the pre-Christian aspects of Mexican culture, will gracefully adorn any wall.

Level of difficulty: Intermediate

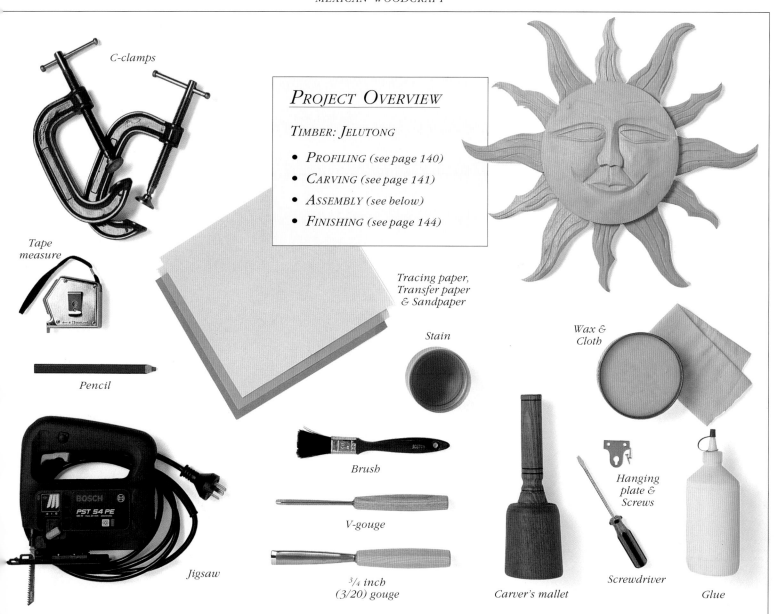

C-clamps

PROJECT OVERVIEW

TIMBER: JELUTONG

- PROFILING (see page 140)
- CARVING (see page 141)
- ASSEMBLY (see below)
- FINISHING (see page 144)

Tape measure

Tracing paper,
Transfer paper
& Sandpaper

Stain

Wax &
Cloth

Pencil

Brush

Hanging
plate &
Screws

Jigsaw

V-gouge

³/₄ inch
(3/20) gouge

Carver's mallet

Screwdriver

Glue

WOODWORKING STEP-BY-STEP

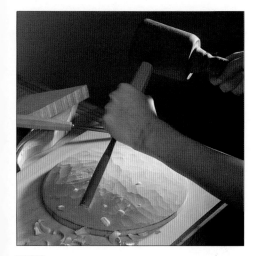

1 Transfer patterns (page 164) so all rays have the same grain direction. Profile rays with a jigsaw and taper them, leaving the center wedge unshaped. Carve three grooves on each and chamfer edges.

2 Cut a disk for the face and mount the disk on to a backboard to make handling easier. Clamp the backboard to the bench. Rough out a dome shape with the carving gouge (see page 141).

3 Transfer the face design on to the dome (see page 133) and carve out the features of the face using the gouge and the V-tool. The carving should not be perfect; a naive style is more suitable.

4 Using a fine sandpaper, sand the background areas and the carved features of the face (see page 144), then remove the face from the backboard.

5 Sand and assemble the rays so that they match the diagram opposite. Glue the spokes of the rays together and then glue the face on top of the rays.

6 Dent the area around the face with a piece of brick or a set of keys (see below). Screw a hanging plate on the back. Stain and wax as desired to finish.

DAMAGING

Several of the projects in this book have been finished to give an impression of age and wear. Painted timber can be distressed lightly with wet-and-dry paper. For a heavier damage, dent unpainted timber with sharp objects, such as a section of brick or a set of keys, and then smooth the dents slightly with sandpaper.

DETAILED VIEW

Face

Rays

ISLAMIC FRETWORK

ISLAMIC DESIGN IS RENOWNED for its profuse ornamentation, rich and lustrous coloring, and its non-representational style which emerged from the prophetic tradition that life like designs should come only from the hand of Allah. Although designs are stylised rather than representational, they still retain exact proportions. The resplendence of Islamic design reflects the divine beauty of Allah and enriches the quality of everyday life.

Fretwork shutter

Islamic fretwork is the focus of the decoration in this 18th century Moroccan palace.

Countries around the world, including Spain, Indonesia, Iran, Iraq, India, Egypt, Morocco and many other areas throughout Northern Africa, have benefited from the influences of Islamic design. The primary focus is on the adorning of functional objects rather than on making objects which are purely decorative.

Islamic fretwork screens have evolved as the perfect solution to the problems of the hot, dry climate which is typical of most of the Islamic countries. They allow air to move quite freely across separated areas of the home, as well as a spread of gentle light, and preserve the privacy which is so essential in a culture where the segregation of the two genders is an central concern. *Mashrabiya*, the Egyptian term for this form of screen, is said to stem from *shariba* which means "to drink," so suggests "drinking in the coolness" in both a metaphorical and a literal sense.

Islamic fret designs arose from a fascination with ancient Greek fret patterns. Fretwork at its finest is a form of three-dimensional carving, in which a series of turned or carved wooden pegs are linked together in one of numerous fret patterns to form the latticed screen. The patterns have the eternal lure of the maze or the labyrinth, in which each item stands alone yet appears to be inextricably woven into the overall design. The arabesque is one renowned form of this pattern. It depicts a continuous vegetal stem which is regularly split to produce offshoots which can, in turn, split. Each separate strand of the pattern eventually returns to be re-included as a part of the main stem.

If a principal motif (*qtib*) would leave large areas undecorated, it is filled in with one of the four main types of decoration: straight-sided polygon motifs *(tastir)*; curved floral or vegetal motifs, *(tawriq)*, or a tree motif *(tashjir)* including arabesques; stylized calligraphy; or filling elements, such as a simple pattern created by pricking with the point of a sharp tool, or the more complex honeycomb of hexagons.

Fretwork sandalwood box

99

DESIGNS AND VARIATIONS

Almost all Islamic areas share the same extremely hot, dry climate, and many of them are desert areas. In such extreme conditions, lush vegetation is readily seen as a symbol of paradise. The leaf, the vine, flowers and other vegetation are therefore prevalent motifs in Islamic decoration, whether carved or inlaid into wood or painted on to the surface.

DESIGNS
Stylized vegetal designs are inspired by real world objects such as almonds, ears of grain and pine cones.

DECORATION
Plaits or borders (Dfira) are used to separate two differently decorated areas.

TIMBERS
Cedar, sandalwood, mahogany, African ebony, and red pine are among the woods used throughout the Islamic world.

Red pine

MOTIFS
Variations on Solomon's seal (the Star of David) form a popular basis for many fretwork motifs.

Sandalwood

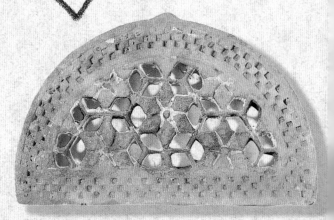

FRETWORK TABLE-TOP
Although most commonly used in screens, partitions and enclosed balconies, Islamic fretwork is also used in furniture.

DECORATED SHUTTERS
A fundamental characteristic of all Islamic decoration is that no large surface areas are left free from ornamentation.

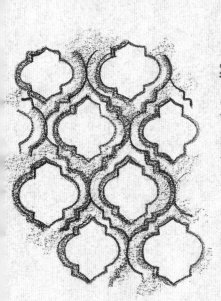

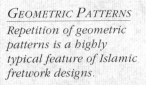

GEOMETRIC PATTERNS
Repetition of geometric patterns is a highly typical feature of Islamic fretwork designs.

MIRROR
This mirror with fretwork surrounds is one possible variation on the mirror project for this chapter.

101

PROJECT: FRETWORK MIRROR

To the Western mind, Islamic culture is something enticing which never fully reveals itself. This discreetly covered mirror hints at that exotic combination. The decorative doweling shown could also be used on a plain picture frame.

Level of difficulty: Advanced

C-clamps

PROJECT OVERVIEW

TIMBER: NEW GUINEA CEDAR & WANGE

- FRET-SAWING (see page 138)
- CUTTING MITERS (see page 138)
- ASSEMBLY (see below)
- MAKING DOWELS (see overleaf)
- FINISHING (see page 144)

Tenon saw

Tape measure

Ruler   Pencil

Miter box

Tracing paper,
Transfer paper &
Sandpaper

Power drill

Splines,
Keys or
Biscuits

Cloth & Stain

Glue

Oil

Hanging
wire

6 x #6 x ¹/₂ inch flat
head wood screws

Eyelets

Jigsaw

Half-round file

Screwdriver

WOODWORKING STEP-BY-STEP

1 Cut the timber to size. Transfer pattern (page 165) on to the 15³/₄ x 23⁵/₈ inch (400 x 600 mm) board, leaving a third of the board free for clamping. Mark design to be cut.

2 Drill a hole in the center of each cutout. Clamp the board on to a piece of scrap wood so as not to fray the underside of the timber when cutting.

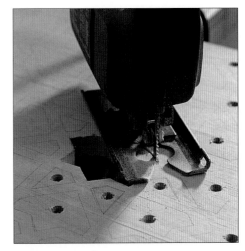

3 Cut the fretwork design with a jigsaw, starting in the center and working out. Swivel the board around before cutting out the other half.

4 Smooth edges of the cut outs with a file and sand the surface on both sides of the board. Cut around fretwork to a 15³/₄ x 15³/₄ inch (400 x 400 mm) size. Stain and oil.

5 Cut the miters for the frames and rout a mortise in each mitered end. Cover spline or key with glue, insert into mortise, ease the connecting piece in place.

6 Form the two frames separately and stain the inside one. Join the two frames, forming a rabbet for the mirror, then fix with screws from the back.

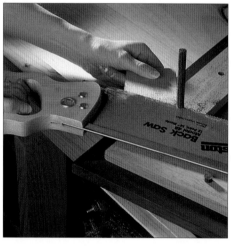

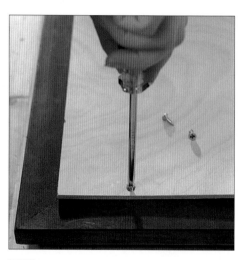

7 Drill holes in the center of the front frame at 4⁹/₁₆ inch (115 mm) intervals and plug with decorative dowel. Cut the dowel using a piece of plywood as a buffer and then sand to the level of the frame.

8 Insert fretwork and mirror into the rabbet. Position backing plywood and fix with screws. Stain and oil the back. Attach two eye hooks into the back of the frame and attach a wire for hanging.

MAKING DOWELS

Although ready-made dowels are available, when you want dowels that closely match the timber being used you can make your own from a suitable softwood. A piece of angle iron is used to make a template. Drill a hole through the angle iron using a drill bit slightly larger than the size of the required piece of dowel. This drilling creates a funnel in the iron which forms a blade. Pieces of timber which have been roughly cut to size are then hammered through the hole with a mallet and the rough, uneven edges are shaved off by the metal. The result is uniform sized dowels.

DETAILED VIEW

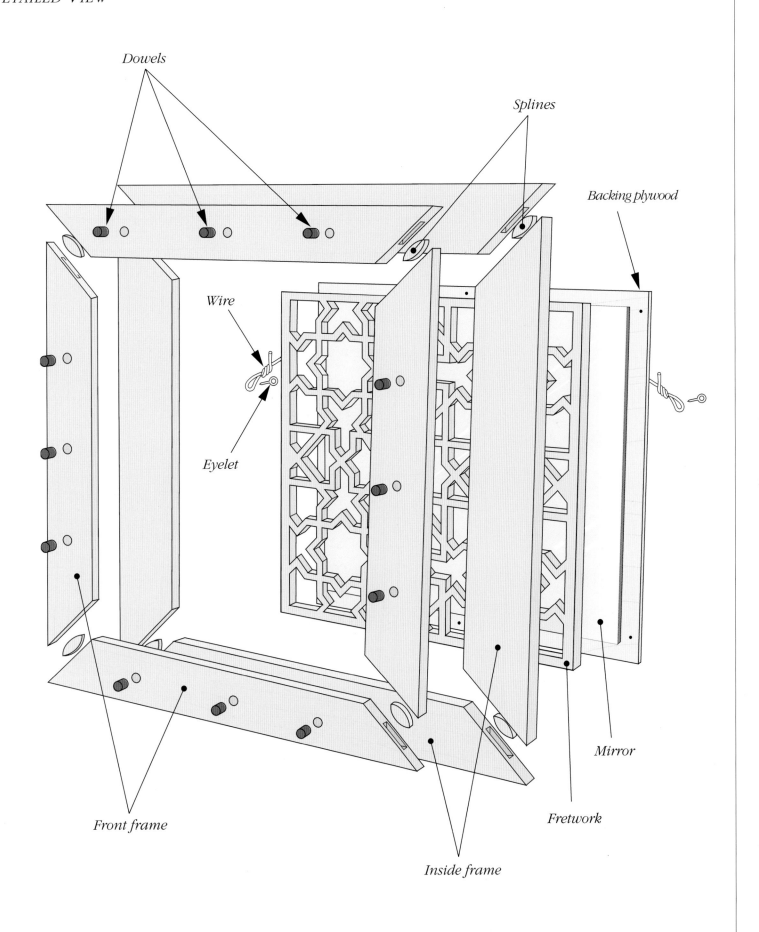

Dowels

Splines

Backing plywood

Wire

Eyelet

Front frame

Inside frame

Fretwork

Mirror

PROJECT: FRETWORK TABLE

Two fretwork designs are featured on this small hexagonal table:
a star on the top and a chain pattern on the skirts of the table. If
you prefer a less decorative appearance, the design could be
simplified by omitting the fretwork from the skirts.

Level of difficulty: Advanced

Handsaw

C-clamps

Tape measure

Pencil

Ruler

Hand plane

*Tracing paper,
Transfer paper &
Sandpaper*

Glue

*Half-
round
file*

Nails

Screwdriver

Oil & Cloth

*24 x #8 x
1¹/₄ inch flat
head wood
screws*

Jigsaw

Router

Power drill

Hammer

Orbital sander

PROJECT OVERVIEW

TIMBER: NEW GUINEA CEDAR

- *LAMINATING (see page 18)*
- *FRETWORK (see below)*
- *ROUTING (see page 139)*
- *ASSEMBLY (see below)*
- *FINISHING (see page 144)*

WOODWORKING STEP-BY-STEP

1 Cut timber to size (see page 166). Laminate pieces to form table-top and cut to shape, along with shelf. Transfer fretwork patterns on to table-top and skirts.

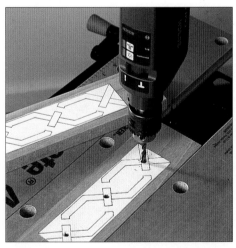

2 Mark the sections of fretwork to be cut out, and drill a hole in each of the cutouts. The hole needs to be large enough to fit the jigsaw blade through.

3 Insert the jigsaw blade into the hole and then carefully cut out each of the shapes, using the patterns you have transferred on to the timber (see page 138).

4 Smooth off the edges of each of the cut outs with a round file and sand both sides. Miter the ends of each skirt to 60° angle, using miter box and tenon saw.

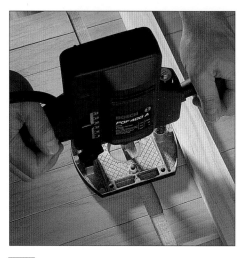

5 Clamp legs together, rout a ¼ inch (6 mm) deep housing. Cut 6 plywood rectangles slightly smaller than the skirts. Glue plywood to back of skirts with best side showing.

6 Taper the lower half of each leg with an orbital sander (leave them plain if you prefer). Screw two legs on to each skirt to construct six leg sections.

7 Rout the underside of the table-top to create a mortised joint (see page 143 for more details). Position each of the leg sections into the table-top and glue.

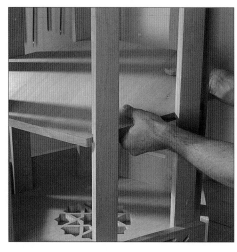

8 Lower the shelf into routed groove and secure the shelf by hammering a nail in at each leg. Punch the nail heads below the surface and putty the hole.

9 Glue the edge strips around the edges of the table-top and chamfer them with a hand plane (see page 141). Sand and oil to complete the table.

DETAILED VIEW

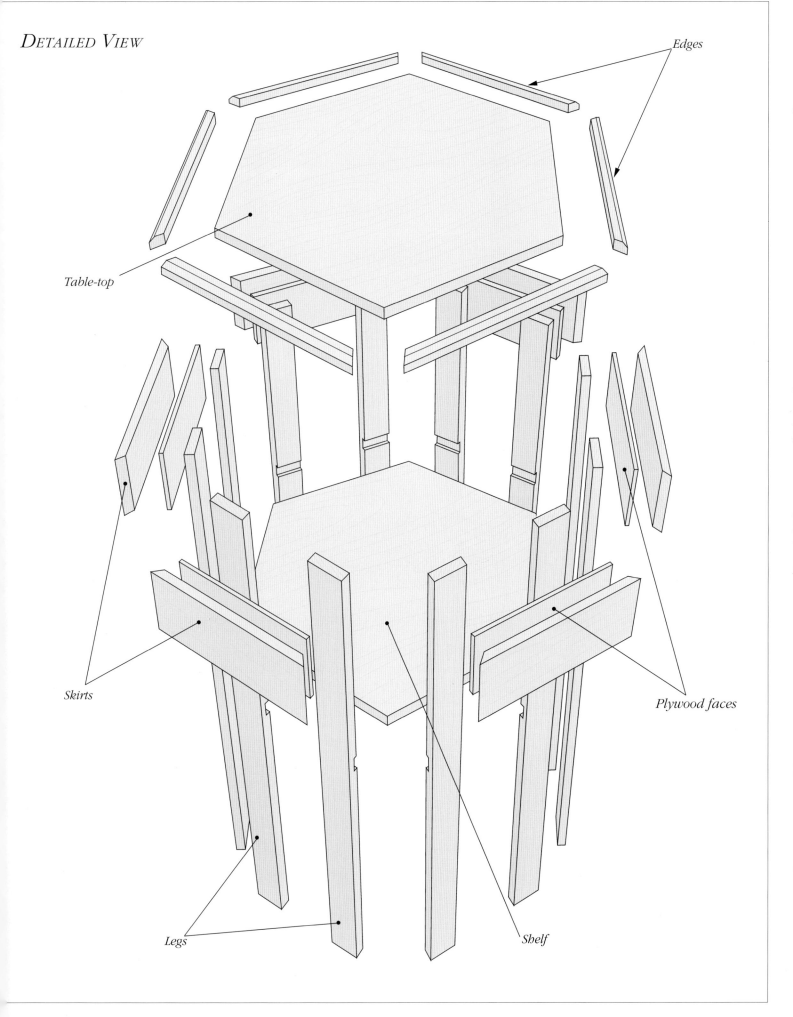

Edges

Table-top

Skirts

Plywood faces

Legs

Shelf

JAPANESE WOOD ART

JAPANESE WOODCRAFTS have a long history which has given rise to a tradition of superbly made tools and techniques. In Japan, the worker of wood is expected to bring out the individual character of the natural material and create from it something that will be both used and treasured for centuries to come. Japanese wooden items convey a harmony with nature plus the sense of a craft faithfully performed.

Lacquerware cups

The archipelago of Japan runs long and narrow from arctic regions in the north to a tropical south. Two-thirds of the country is covered by forests that support seven hundred indigenous varieties of tree. The volcanic soil of the area yields little for the mason, so Japan's architecture has naturally developed around timber rather than stone. Even before the tools which were needed to fashion wooden artifacts were developed, softwood timber was split length-wise and woven into boxes, tables and the like. Between the third and fourth centuries, woodcraft skills reached Japan from Korea. Several centuries later, as Buddhism began to flourish in Japan, a demand for wooden statues kept sculptors busy.

Sculptors worked in maple, camphorwood and zelkova and, following the trend of imitating the Chinese style, decorated their pieces in a gaudy manner. A 'pure' Japanese style emerged with the introduction of Zen Buddhism in the thirteenth century, when the sumptuous Chinese aesthetic gave way to a more elegant, simple and sturdy one.

Woodwork may be unvarnished, in the style of *shoji* screens and other household fittings, or they may be finished with polished lacquer. Lacquered objects commonly include tea ceremony shelves and tables, *hako* chests, and trousseau objects such as *haribako*, or sewing boxes. The design of all these items avoids excess wherever possible. They are fashioned from paulownia, zelkova, and mulberry woods, or from exotic timbers such as ebony and red sandalwood.

Bento box

The focus of carving eventually shifted away from formal sculpture towards small, finely-wrought items such as tobacco boxes, dolls and *netsuke* or miniature sculptures. Attention to detail and to the raw material remain as basic tenets.

Lamp decorated with flowers of the four seasons.

The front steps and balcony of the Nezu shrine near Ueno are elaborately carved and painted.

DESIGNS AND VARIATIONS

Daiku, the Japanese word for a person who designs and makes things in wood, means "chief artisan." The natural beauty and individuality of the wood is enhanced, never destroyed, by the techniques of Japanese woodcraft. Correct proportion (*kiwari*) is of particular significance in achieving the ideal design. Decorations are inspired by nature and the elements. Japanese wood working tools such as the saw and plane cut on the pull stroke, rather than the push stroke.

TABLEWARE
Miso bowls are used for serving a hot broth style of soup. Wood from conifers and broad leaf trees is used. Layers of lacquer are applied to seal the wood.

LACQUERWARE
Lacquer is made from the sap of the urushi *tree. It is used for its protective, decorative and adhesive qualities.*

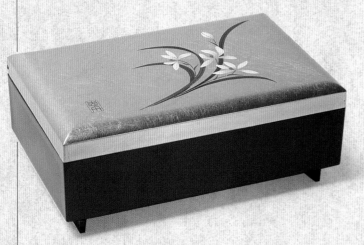

STANDING TRAY
The serving trays in the project can be varied by the addition of legs which can be hinged to fold away when not in use.

COLORS
The sap of the urushi *tree is mixed with carbon to produce a pitch black color, or with cinnabar for a bright red lacquer.*

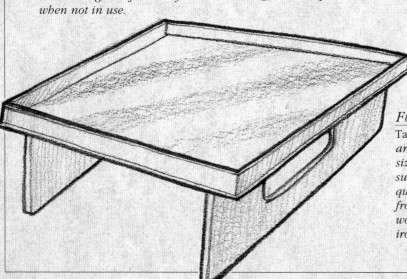

FURNITURE
Tansu chests, which are built in varied sizes and shapes to suit small living quarters, are made from richly grained woods with black ironwork trimmings.

Japanese oak

Cypress pine

Sen

TIMBERS
Other popular timbers include hinoki *(cypress),* koyomaki *(parasol fir) and* sugi *(cedar). Bamboo is used to make strong, attractive, light-weight pieces.*

SHOJI STYLE
Rice paper and bamboo are combined to make lamps, screens and sliding doors in the Shoji *style.*

JOINTS
Japanese joinery employs intricate and inventive shapes and designs. Ai-gaki *the cross lap joint pictured above is one of the types of joints used for the intersection of slats in* shoji *pieces.*

Project: Japanese Serving Trays

Japanese joinery is a highly developed art form which involves clever and intricate shaping. Traditionally, these *bon* or serving trays would be made with mitered open mortises or stop butt housing joints. These trays are usually lacquered with a black or a terracotta color.

Level of difficulty: Intermediate

Ruler Pencil

Hand
saw

Project Overview

TIMBERS: SILVER ASH & PLYWOOD

- ROUTING (see page 139)
- CUTTING MITERS (see page 138)
- ASSEMBLY (see below)
- LACQUERING (see page 116)
- FINISHING (see page 144)

Tracing paper,
Transfer paper
& Sandpaper

Masking
tape

Tape
measure

Miter
box

Router

Varnish

Putty

Brads

Tack
hammer

Pickling
solution

Brush

Glue

WOODWORKING STEP-BY-STEP

1 Cut the timber for the side pieces to the specified width (see page 167). Rout a ¹/₄ x ¹/₄ inch (6 x 6 mm) rabbet along the full length of the timber for the side.

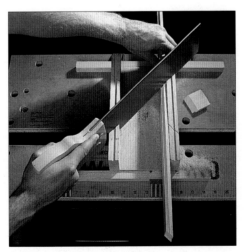

2 Place the length for the side pieces into the miter box and cut, with 45° miters, to the required lengths for each of the various side pieces (see page 138).

3 Glue the sides and secure with masking tape, measure that the diagonals are of equal lengths. For extra strength you can secure with brads.

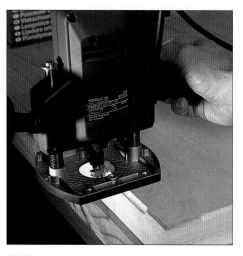

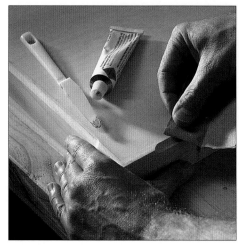

| 4 | Cut the plywood to fit the rabbet and glue it in place. To secure it, half sink the panel pins leaving the heads exposed. Remove pins when the glue dries. |

4 Cut the plywood to fit the rabbet and glue it in place. To secure it, half sink the panel pins leaving the heads exposed. Remove pins when the glue dries.

5 Use a ¼ inch (6.5 mm) cove bit on the router to rout the base of the sides, starting and finishing 1 inch (25 mm) from each corner (see page 139). This creates the illusion of legs.

6 Fill any cracks and panel pin holes with a light-colored filler. Sand to a fine finish (see page 144), then paint and lacquer (see below) to complete.

LACQUERING

You can imitate the rich sheen of Japanese lacquerwork by applying many coats of varnish over a smoothly painted surface. Wipe the object with a tack cloth to remove dust. Apply up to ten coats of varnish with a flat brush, fine sanding between coats and leaving the piece to dry in a dust-free environment.

Detailed View

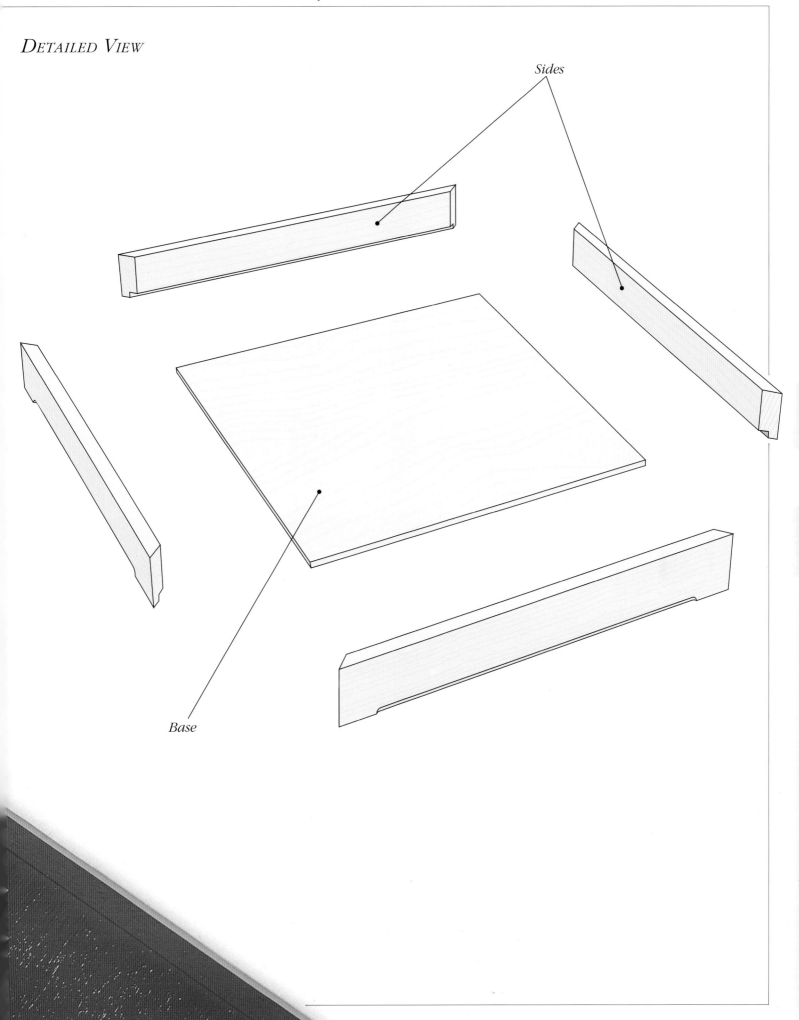

Sides

Base

PROJECT: JAPANESE SCREEN

This folding screen is a variation on the traditional *shoji*, room partitions covered in a translucent paper which lets light through but prevents drafts. Cutting the numerous cross laps requires a little patience and care, but the results are well worthwhile.

Level of difficulty: Advanced

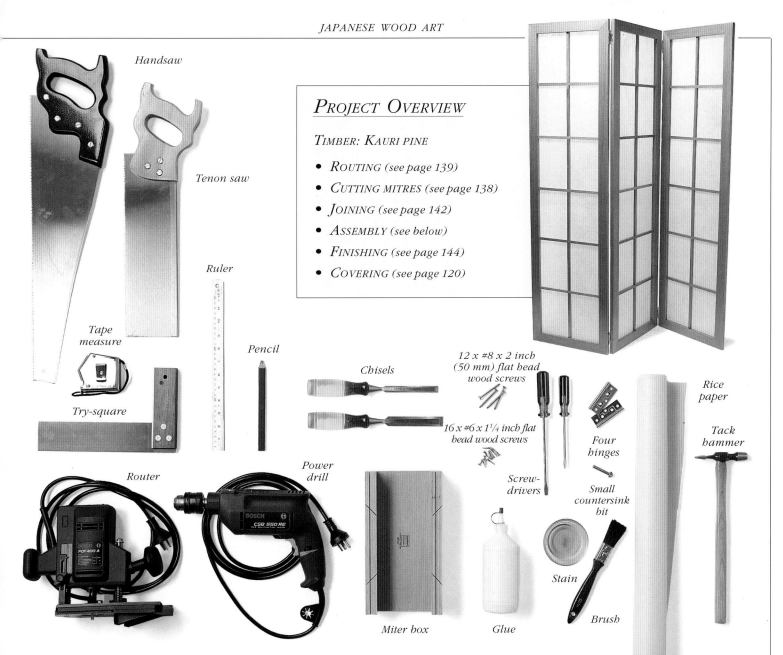

Handsaw

Tenon saw

Ruler

Tape measure

Pencil

Try-square

PROJECT OVERVIEW

TIMBER: KAURI PINE

- *ROUTING (see page 139)*
- *CUTTING MITRES (see page 138)*
- *JOINING (see page 142)*
- *ASSEMBLY (see below)*
- *FINISHING (see page 144)*
- *COVERING (see page 120)*

Chisels

12 x #8 x 2 inch (50 mm) flat head wood screws

16 x #6 x 1¼ inch flat head wood screws

Screwdrivers

Four hinges

Small countersink bit

Rice paper

Tack hammer

Router

Power drill

Miter box

Glue

Stain

Brush

WOODWORK STEP-BY-STEP

1 Cut struts to required size (see page 167). Miter the ends of the frame pieces and the cover strips to 45° angles (see page 138). Glue all the mitered joints.

2 Rout a ½ x ½ inch (12 x 12 mm) rabbet along one edge of each frame piece(see page 139). Drill pilot holes entering from the top and base and secure with 2 inch (50 mm) screws.

3 Check internal measurements of the frame and trim all struts to fit. Use a knife or pencil to mark out housings ¼ inch (6 mm) deep at equal intervals along the struts.

4 Using the tenon saw and a ¹/₂ inch (12 mm) chisel, cut housings into the struts for the cross pieces, then lay the horizontal struts in position in the frame.

5 With the housings facing upwards, place the vertical struts in position, mark for correct sizes. Remove the struts and trim the housings if necessary.

6 Reassemble, adding glue to each joint. Tack the outer struts to the routed frame using the panel pins. Finish all of the timber at this point.

7 Cover the panels with fabric or rice paper, fixing in place with glue, a staple gun or tacks, as appropriate. Trim the covering to size so that edges will be concealed by the cover strip.

8 Tack all of the cover strips on to the frame using a panel pin at each of the intersections. Hinge all of the frames together, using 1¹/₄ inch (20 mm) screws and a hinge at the top and bottom between panels.

Many fibrous materials are suitable for covering the screen, including paper and polyester lining fabric.

DETAILED VIEW

Frame top

Horizontal struts

Vertical struts

Cover strips

Frame sides

Frame base

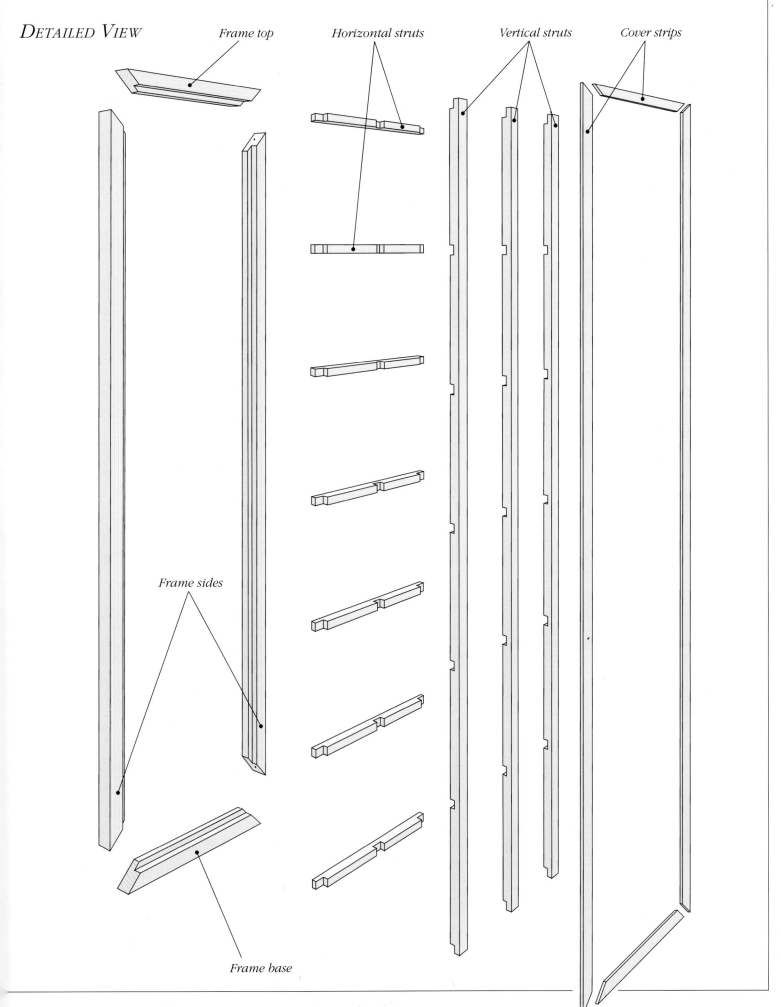

AUSTRALIAN COLONIAL

WHEN THE EARLY WHITE SETTLERS ARRIVED in Australia, their most urgent priority was to become self sufficient. The vast distances that separated Terra Australis from the settlers' source of supplies meant that they had to quickly adapt to the unfamiliar climate, landscape and materials at hand. The settlers worked tirelessly and inventively to create a style of woodcraft that is as diverse and subtle as the raw beauty of the Australian bush.

Pull-along horse

A wide variety of rustic styles, including packing case, slab and stick furniture, are typical of Australian Colonial woodcraft. Styles which use timber in its raw state and require more skill in assembly than in the cutting and shaping of wood. Forked branches were sliced in two to form the legs of a stick chair, gnarled roots were used as pedestals for slab-top stools and rough-hewn sapling poles were used for the frame for a bush home.

Speed was essential so there was initially little or no finishing. Chairs were made in varied and unusual styles, from the simplest log stool, to the ingenious *squatter's delight* which consisted of just two battens and two cross pieces with sacking for the seat, it required the side of a house or a tree trunk for support. The more affluent settlers reclined on a squatter's chair. The Jimmy Possum chair was built with angled, tapered legs extending through the seat base to form the arm supports.

Foodsafes were modified to suit the demands of bush life. The legs were elongated and placed in tins of water to protect the food from insects and wildlife. Screen, hand-punched metal, louvers or lattice with fabric backing allowed airflow and kept out pests.

Packing cases and crates were used to make chair seats, drawers, and many other house-hold items. Even humble cotton spools were used to make handles, finials and decorations, or glued together to make battens for whatnots, which were used to display ornaments.

Whatnot

As the focus moved from survival to comfort and aesthetics, pieces were finished or decorated. Spattric, or splatter work, was employed to decorate dressers, sideboards and chests. Pyrography, or pokerwork, was popular, with patterns inspired by the local bush flora and fauna. More skilled woodworkers used the contrasts inherent in local timbers to make exquisite decorative inlays.

Rough textures and unfinished logs are typical of Australian bush style.

Grinder on a plank-and-log table

DESIGNS AND VARIATIONS

Australian Colonial woodwork is characterized by ingenuity and practicality. Necessity was truly the mother of invention, as many of the highly innovative styles of woodcraft demonstrate. Australian hardwoods are much more difficult to work than European timbers, and many settlers' tools were blunted or broken. This is perhaps why styles focused on using the timber in its raw state. Although brittle, the local timbers are durable and develop an excellent patina over time.

CUTLERY TRAY
This simple but effective tray was used for storage and to carry the cutlery to the outdoor table.

DIE STAMP
The renowned kangaroo design from the Melbourne Chair Company. Other designs featured the emu and the lyre bird.

TIMBERS
The isolation of Colonial Australia meant that mostly local, rather than imported, timbers were used.

CHEST
The drawers of this chest from Tasmania consist of boxes which once transported ammunition.

Australian red cedar

Jarrah

Tasmanian blackwood

Huon pine

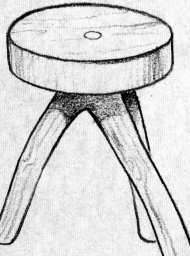

SLAB STOOL
The seat of this stool is made from a slab of wood which is pinned with a dowel to the forked branch legs.

CARVING
Unique local flora and fauna provide many delightful sources of inspiration for the Australian craftsperson.

SQUATTER'S CHAIR
An adjustable canvas back allowed the Squatter to recline in comfort with legs dangling over the extended arms of the chair.

FOOD SAFE
Food safe panels of mesh provide airflow and protection from vermin.

BUSH CHAIR
The natural shape of timber was put to great use in making more primitive but functional furniture in the bush.

SHEARER'S CHAIR
Also known as the miner's chair, this fold-up chair was made for wandering workers.

JIMMY POSSUM
This stick chair takes its name from a Tasmanian tradesman whose style of chair was adopted throughout Australia.

PROJECT: COLONIAL FOOD SAFE

Preserving food in a warm climate was once a serious problem for
Australians. The punched holes in the tin sides of a food safe were
designed to allow air in and to keep flies and vermin out. If ants
were a problem, the legs were set in dishes of water.

Level of difficulty: Advanced

Handsaw

Marking gauge

Tenon saw

Tape measure

Pencil

Ruler

Hand drill

PROJECT OVERVIEW

TIMBER: KAURI PINE

- JOINTS (see page 142)
- ASSEMBLY (see below)
- PUNCHING TIN (see page 128)
- JIGSAWING (see page 139)
- FINISHING (see page 144)

Tracing paper, Transfer paper & Sandpaper

Nail for punching

Carpenter's chisels

Wax & Cloth

Tin snips

Hammer

Screwdriver

8 x #6 x ¾ inch (10 mm) flat head wood screws

Hinges

Glue

2 x #12 x 1½ inch (40 mm) flat head wood screws

Flat head tacks

Jigsaw

C-clamps

Hand plane

WOODWORKING STEP-BY-STEP

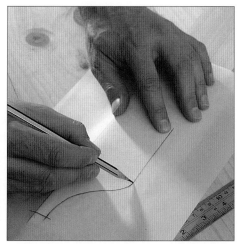

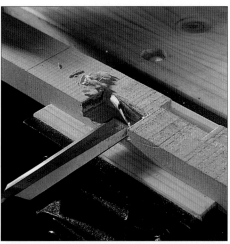

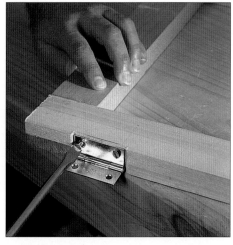

1 Cut timber to size (see page 138). Transfer the patterns for the splashback and sides. Scribe the housed joints using a sharp pencil or a knife.

2 Using a tenon saw and chisel, cut joints A and B (tee half lap joints, see page 142). To cut joint C (stopped half lap joint) you will only need the chisel.

3 Assemble the body frame. Assemble the door frame and lightly clamp the pieces together. Screw the hinges in place on the inside of the door using the ¾ inch screws.

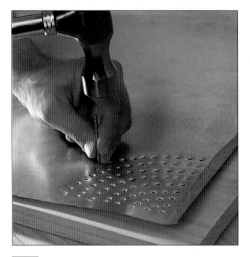

4 Plane the door frame so that it fits the body loosely. Attach the top and base to the body frame and glue them into position. Lightly clamp together until dry.

5 Cut the tin to size. Punch the pattern on the inside of each piece of tin. Place the decorated tin on each of the frames and use flat head tacks to attach.

6 Glue the cleats in position inside the food safe and tack them for a firm hold. Position the shelf on the cleats and then screw the door in place.

7 Cut the splashback and sides with a jigsaw (see page 139). Glue it into place around the top and weight it firmly with bricks until the glue sets.

8 Using the 1$\frac{1}{2}$ inch (40 mm) flat head screws, fix the block of wood for the latch on to the frame, the other screw is left jutting out. Wax and distress as required to finish.

PUNCHING

Use a piece of scrap timber to rest the metal on for punching the holes in. A large nail should be used for punching the holes. You can draw the design on to the metal first so that you will not have to keep referring to the pattern. The metal is put in place in the panels with the raised side of the holes facing out of the cupboard to stop insects from crawling in.

DETAILED VIEW

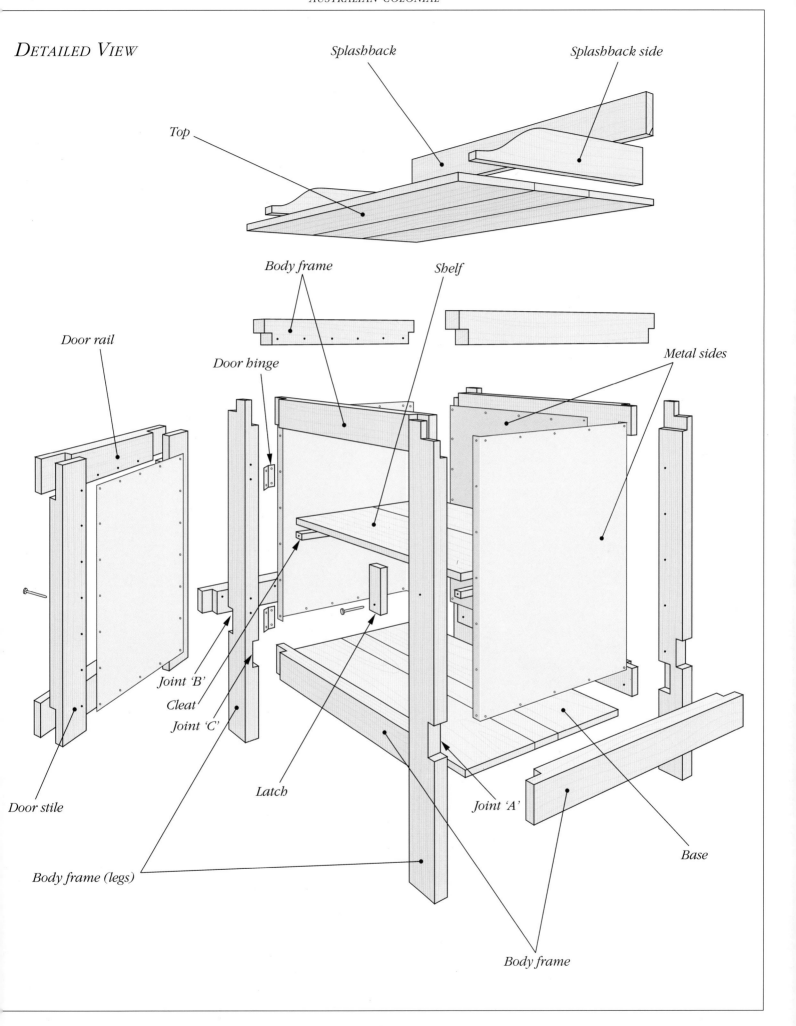

Splashback

Splashback side

Top

Body frame

Shelf

Door rail

Door hinge

Metal sides

Joint 'B'

Cleat

Joint 'C'

Latch

Joint 'A'

Door stile

Body frame (legs)

Base

Body frame

PROJECT: COLONIAL CUTLERY TRAY

A sturdy portable tray, with sections for cutlery, usually sat on the Australian kitchen dresser. The cut-out handle enabled it to be easily carried outside to the table before each meal time. This one has been painted green and distressed to give an appearance of age.

Level of difficulty: Beginner

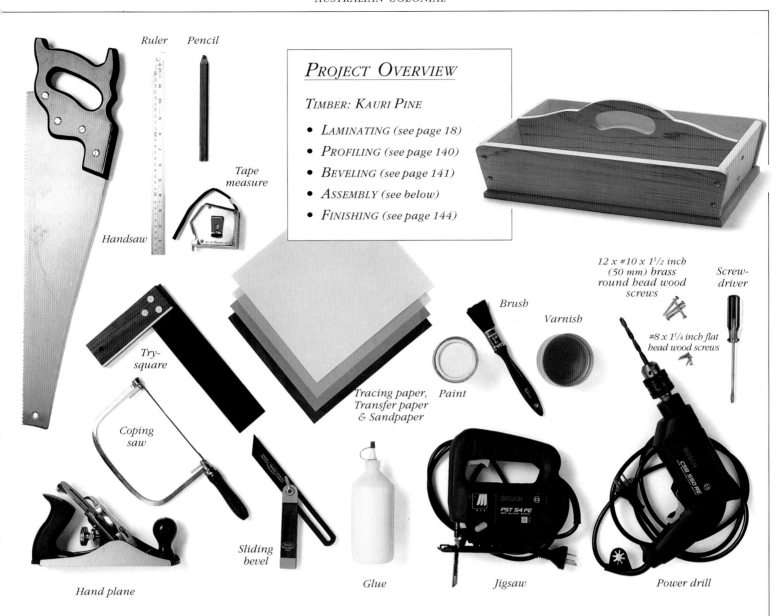

Ruler   *Pencil*

Tape measure

Handsaw

PROJECT OVERVIEW

TIMBER: KAURI PINE

- LAMINATING (see page 18)
- PROFILING (see page 140)
- BEVELING (see page 141)
- ASSEMBLY (see below)
- FINISHING (see page 144)

Try-square

Coping saw

Tracing paper, Transfer paper & Sandpaper

Paint

Brush

Varnish

12 x #10 x 1½ inch (50 mm) brass round head wood screws

Screw-driver

#8 x 1¼ inch flat head wood screws

Sliding bevel

Hand plane

Glue

Jigsaw

Power drill

WOODWORKING STEP-BY-STEP

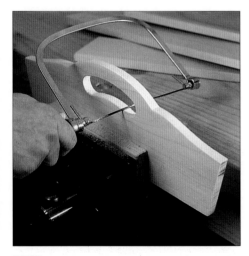

1   Cut pieces to length (see page 170). Laminate two pieces to form a base. Transfer the pattern for the sides and handle and profile with a jigsaw. Drill two holes on the handle and fret-saw the hand hole.

2   Bevel the bottom edge of each of the two side pieces to an angle of 10°. Chamfer around the top edge of the base for decoration (see page 141). Sand all of the pieces, then assemble and glue.

3   Drill holes at an angle through the base and into the sides. Countersink brass screws. Drill holes at ends and fix handle in place with round head brass screws. Paint, distress, and varnish.

GENERAL INFORMATION

THIS CHAPTER WILL BE OF PARTICULAR USE to the beginning woodworker who may need some more details on how to carry out the steps for each of the projects in the book. There are details on each of the main techniques required. As you gain more experience you will be able to customize the projects and add your own individual touches using the Designs and Variations spreads in each chapter for inspiration.

CHOOSING TIMBERS

Timbers are classified as being either softwood or hardwood. This terminology can be a little confusing because it sometimes does not indicate the actual physical softness or hardness of a timber, for example balsa wood is classed as a hardwood although it is actually "soft" to handle. For details about the various

Always measure carefully before cutting your timber.

timbers which can be used in the projects refer to the catalogue of timbers which begins on page 146.

Hardwoods are those timbers which come from broad-leaved trees such as oak, mahogany, eucalyptus and maple. These trees produce seeds which form inside a ripening fruit. Their timbers are close-grained and have open vessels known as pores, they are therefore called "porous woods." The close grain helps to prevent the wood from splintering but means that the wood is often more difficult for beginners to work with. Pieces made from hardwoods will last well for hundreds of years if they are properly finished and cared for.

Softwoods come from conifers, evergreen trees which produce their seeds uncovered, usually in cone-like structures. Softwoods do not have pores and are called non-porous. They usually have a large, open grain which means they are easier to use for sawing, carving and nailing. With the exception of most pine timbers, softwoods are inclined to split and splinter if used for intricate pieces. As softwoods are not as durable as hardwoods, they last best if finished with paint or varnish rather than just a wax finish.

Timber is classed according to its quality. The two classifications used are "select" and "common." Select timber is usually used for furniture making and is the better quality, more expensive timber. It comes in grades of A, B and C, where A is the most perfect timber and C will have some small defects, for example knots or a very varied coloring. Common timber is most frequently used by builders and is graded from 1 to 4, where 1 is the best quality common timber and 4 is an extremely rough, knotty timber used for making crates. To save money you can occasionally work with a mixture of select and common timber, using the better quality where it will be visible and the rougher classes where the timber will not be seen.

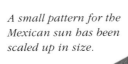

*A small pattern for the
Mexican sun has been
scaled up in size.*

RE-USING TIMBERS

Old timbers can be re-used to make pieces. It is
often relatively simple and sometimes cheap to
pick up used timbers from building demolishers,
garage sales and junk shops. Occasionally you
will be lucky enough to find some more unusual
timbers second-hand which are no longer
readily available in the lumber yards. When
re-using old timbers, take care with preparing
the timber and puttying any defects.

TRANSFERRING PATTERNS

The easiest method for enlarging a pattern is to use
a photocopying machine that can enlarge by the
required percentage. If you are not able to do this,
you can first transfer the design on to tracing paper
and draw a grid over it, numbering each square of
the grid. Take another piece of tracing paper which is
large enough to draw the pattern at actual size. Draw
a larger grid with the same quantity of squares as the
smaller sheet, and number each square to match those on
the original grid. On the larger grid, copy the detail from
the original square by square. The illustration to the right
shows the original pattern which has been traced on to a
grid and behind it the larger grid with the same pattern.

To transfer the design to your timber, place the larger
grid on the timber and secure it in position with masking
tape. Insert a sheet of transfer paper between the tracing
paper and timber with the coated side facing the timber.
Run the end of a stylus firmly over the pattern.

Alternatively, if you feel confident, you can create the
second grid directly on the timber and then draw the
pattern freehand in each square of your grid on the
timber. For larger pieces you will either need to draw
the second grid directly on to the timber or use several
pieces of tracing paper to create the whole design in
separate sections. For symmetrical patterns, you will only
need to draw half of the pattern on to the grid and then
you can flip your tracing over to complete the pattern.

GRAIN

When planing or chiseling timber it is important to work
across or with the grain. Going against the grain will
pluck out the ends of the wood fibers and result in a
broken and rough surface. In the diagram, the shaded
fibers labelled 'A' rise to the surface in such a way that if
you planed them right to left they would break away.
The shaded fibers labelled 'B' will not break
away if planed from right to left as they
rise to the surface in the opposite
direction. So on this board you
would need to plane one half in
one direction and the other half in
the opposite direction to achieve a
perfect surface. In the center of this
board there is no grain "direction".

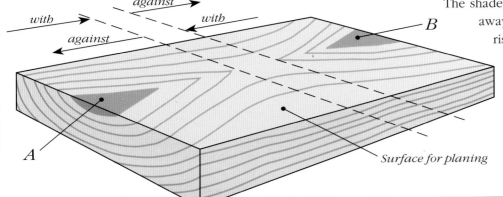

WORKSHOP

When choosing an area to work in you need to ensure that you will be able to get any large pieces of timber in to the workshop and also that you will be able to get finished pieces out, preferably without having to take doors off! The advantages of having the workshop away from the house, in a garage or garden shed, are that noise and dust will not affect the rest of the household.

The workshop area needs to be free from excess moisture which can cause problems with tools. Good lighting and ventilation are necessary for safety purposes as well as for comfort. Natural light is best and can be obtained by using translucent door, ceiling or wall panels if windows are not available. A skylight would also provide an excellent source of natural light. For working on your projects in the evenings, fluorescent lighting is an economical choice, with spot lights for dark areas. All lights should be shielded from flying wood chips.

Power tools require adequate electrical outlets and proper grounding. It is important to ensure that using your tools will not exceed available electrical capacity. If in any doubt, be sure to consult a qualified electrician. Avoid having cables running across the floor or on work areas where they may be damaged by the slip of a tool.

Another vital safety consideration is that of avoiding fire hazards, keep your workshop free of excess sawdust and woodchips, don't allow anyone to smoke in the area, keep flammable paints and varnishes safely stored according to the manufacturer's directions and extinguish any pilot flames before using flammable materials. A fire extinguisher is a worthwhile purchase for the workshop and for the home. Naturally, the entire workshop should be off limits to young children and dangerous substances and materials should be well out of reach and preferably locked away from curious youngsters.

Hand tools should be within easy reach while you are working, but out of the way. Suspending them from hooks or nails on a wall near your bench is probably the best solution. Any tools which are large and heavy should preferably be set up in a place where they can be used without being moved. Allow enough room to be able to work at them using large pieces of timber.

Timber needs to be stored in a place where it is well aired and will not warp. The workbench must be sturdy enough to withstand heavy pieces being manipulated and the vibrations of power tools. You will need some storage capacity for smaller items like nails and screws, this could be drawers or compartmentalized boxes. For finishing you need an area where you can apply the finish and leave the piece standing until dry. A partition or curtain may be needed to protect it from sawdust.

TOOLS

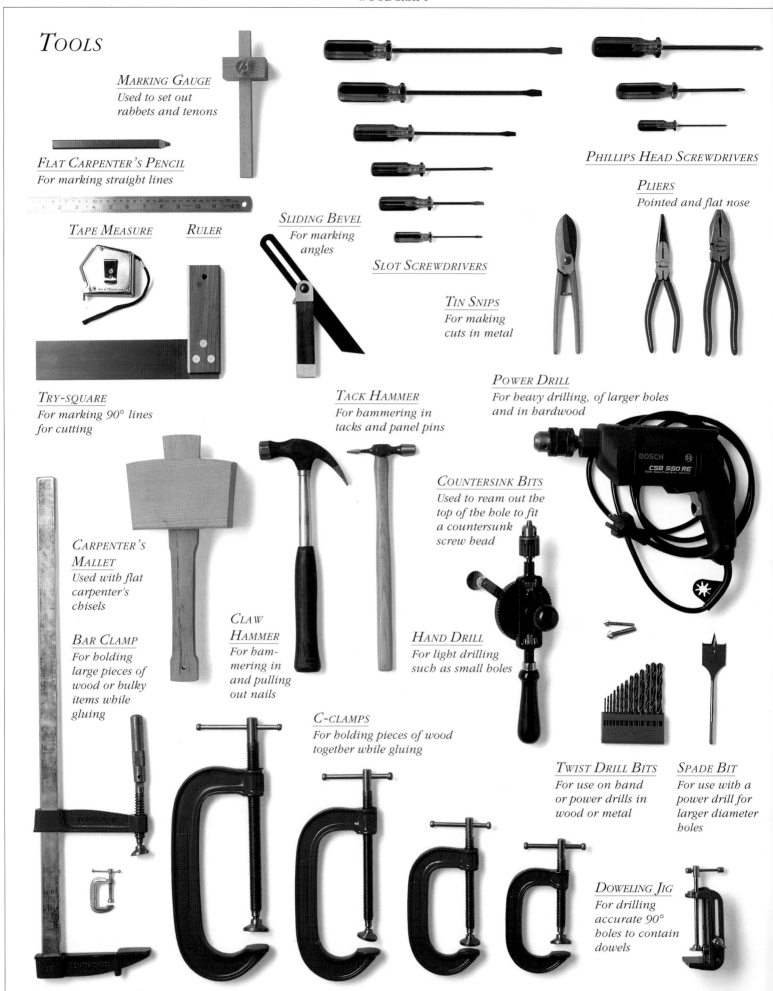

MARKING GAUGE
Used to set out
rabbets and tenons

FLAT CARPENTER'S PENCIL
For marking straight lines

TAPE MEASURE   **RULER**

SLIDING BEVEL
For marking
angles

PHILLIPS HEAD SCREWDRIVERS

PLIERS
Pointed and flat nose

SLOT SCREWDRIVERS

TIN SNIPS
For making
cuts in metal

TRY-SQUARE
For marking 90° lines
for cutting

TACK HAMMER
For hammering in
tacks and panel pins

POWER DRILL
For heavy drilling, of larger holes
and in hardwood

COUNTERSINK BITS
Used to ream out the
top of the hole to fit
a countersunk
screw head

CARPENTER'S MALLET
Used with flat
carpenter's
chisels

CLAW HAMMER
For ham-
mering in
and pulling
out nails

HAND DRILL
For light drilling
such as small holes

BAR CLAMP
For holding
large pieces of
wood or bulky
items while
gluing

C-CLAMPS
For holding pieces of wood
together while gluing

TWIST DRILL BITS
For use on hand
or power drills in
wood or metal

SPADE BIT
For use with a
power drill for
larger diameter
holes

DOWELING JIG
For drilling
accurate 90°
holes to contain
dowels

RASPS
Curved and flat, used to roughly shape edges

SANDING BLOCK
For sanding flat surfaces, wrap paper around block

ORBITAL SANDER
Used to sand large flat surfaces to a fine finish

CARVER'S MALLET
Used together with woodcarving gouges

FILES
For finer finishing; round file used for enlarging holes

HAND SAW
For hand-cutting larger pieces of wood

TENON SAW
Used with a miter box for cutting angles and tenons

CARVING GOUGES
For creating sculpted shapes

ROTARY ORBITAL SANDER
For an extra fine finish

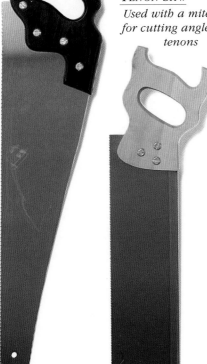

CARPENTER'S CHISELS
For making joins

SPOKESHAVE
For rounding off edges

COPING SAW
For cutting out fine shapes

HAND PLANES
For creating flat surfaces and edges

JIGSAW
For fast cutting of curved shapes

MITER BOX
For accurately cutting angles on strips of timber

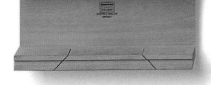

ROUTER
Used with different shaped bits for cutting grooves or molding edges

CUTTING TECHNIQUES

SAWING

One of the most common problems that novice woodworkers experience is not being able to achieve a straight saw cut, this is usually due to having your elbow jutting outwards rather than in towards your body as you are holding the saw. Ensure that your saw is held vertical (i.e. at 90° to the wood) by using a try-square. Always keep your saw blades sharp (use a file to sharpen) and in good working condition.

MITERING

A miter is a 45° diagonal joint made by cutting two pieces of wood which are then fitted together to make a 90° corner. Use a miter box to hold the wood steady and the saw vertical and at the correct horizontal angle. A tenon saw in normally used to cut miters in this manner.

COPE-SAWING

A coping saw, with a narrow fine tooth blade, is used to cut open patterns in woodwork. First use a spade bit to drill a hole in the waste wood to be removed and place the coping saw blade through it, then attach the blade to the metal frame with the teeth pointing forward (down). Practice cutting into corners on a scrap first.

JIGSAWING

A power jigsaw allows fast and accurate cutting of a variety of shapes. Make sure you have the correct blade for the purpose and ensure the blade is in securely and the bottom plate is set at the correct angle (follow the manufacturer's instructions for use). Always make sure the power cord is kept well clear of the blade.

ROUTING

A power router enables you to quickly and accurately make grooves, rabbets and fancy molded edges. Router bits come in a wide variety of shapes and sizes for different applications. Routers are dangerous if misused and serious injuries can be caused. Ensure the router bit is securely in place and practice on scraps first. Always follow the manufacturer's instructions for safe usage and maintenance.

CHISELING

Chisels are used with a carpenter's mallet to chip out large sections of timber to house joints, hinges etc. It is important to chisel with the direction of the grain, or across the grain. Don't chisel against the grain as this can cause the timber to split (see page 133). Always use the chisel with the blade moving in a direction away from your body as a chisel can cause serious damage if it slips while being pounded with a mallet. Clamp the timber to the workbench to hold it steady while you are chiseling.

PROFILING TECHNIQUES

FILING

Files and rasps come in a variety of shapes and
sizes and are used for both rough shaping and
finishing of cuts. Rasps are used to achieve a
better shape, as they remove more wood than
files. There are three basic classes of files:
rough, second-cut and smooth. Round files are
used for enlarging holes. Files are also used to
sharpen the blades of other tools such as saws.
Sandpaper is usually needed for final smoothing
(see page 144 for more details on sanding).

PLANING

A plane is essential if you don't have power
tools and, for smaller tasks, a plane is often
better. There are three basic types of planes: a
block plane (smoothing plane) which is the
smallest, a jack plane (roughing plane), and a
jointer plane (trying plane) which is the longest.
Planing is done on the forward stroke and
should be done in the direction of the grain.

SPOKESHAVING

A spokeshave is a double handled plane used
for planing and shaping curves. Its name comes
from its use in days long past when it was
employed to shape the spokes of wheels. The
spokeshave cuts on both the push and pull
stroke and needs to be used in the direction of
the grain (see page 133) in order to achieve a
smooth, rounded finish. The spokeshave can
also be used to chamfer and round off edges.

BEVELING

Use the sliding bevel to mark bevel angles which are usually other than 90° angles. Set the wing of the tool to the correct angle with a protractor. Lay the sliding bevel on the end of the timber and mark the bevel line in pencil, or with a sharp knife. Plane to this line (see page 140 for details on planing) use the sliding bevel to check that it is even along the length of the line. For 90° angles use a try-square.

CHAMFERING

To chamfer is to remove timber by planing a narrow flat area, usually at an angle of 45° to the main surface. It is done to improve the appearance or to diminish the risk of damage to (and from) sharp corners. Use a small plane to carefully remove the corners. The exact size and angel of the chamfer will depend on the type of appearance required in the finished piece.

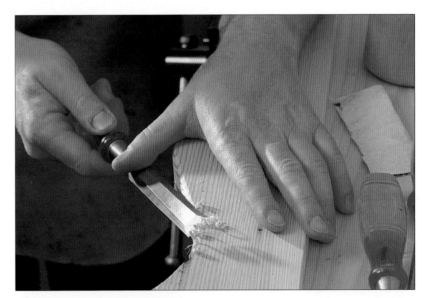

CARVING

Carving is usually done with gouges, which come with a variety of curved or v shaped blades. They are used with a wooden carver's mallet. For a good finish never carve against the grain as this can cause splintering or even splitting of the timber (see page 133). It is safest to clamp the timber to the workbench to hold it steady and to carve with or across the grain, in a direction moving away from your body.

JOINING TECHNIQUES

WEDGED

A wedged joint is used where a long piece is required to be joined to a flat surface, like a leg into a chair seat. The slot for the wedge should not be longer than half the thickness of the other piece, and the wedge should be thick enough to splay the timber to jam it against the sides of the hole.

CROSS LAP

Used for joining sections of framing, it is important to ensure that saw cuts are vertical and chisel work is clean and flat. Mark out the saw cuts with a pencil (or you can use a sharp knife for greater accuracy) and use a tenon saw and a sharp, flat carpenter's chisel.

TEE HALF LAP

Another joint used for joining sections of framing. Do not make the joints greater in depth than half the thickness of the wood, otherwise the surfaces will not be flush with one another. Use a try-square and pencil to mark saw cuts and a marking gauge for the depth of the chisel cut, to ensure everything is square.

MORTISE & TENON

One of the most common joints, used where strength and rigidity are needed in frames. Both the mortise (the hole) and the tenon (the tongue) must be cut carefully as non-square tenons and uneven mortise sides will cause the joint to be loose and make gluing very difficult. Use a tenon saw for tenons and a flat carpenter's chisel to cut the mortises to the right size.

DOWELED

A doweled joint is used to quickly make a strong, rigid join using the minimum of materials. Dowel holes must be vertical to the surface and the dowels must fit closely in the holes. Glue is put on the end of the dowel and into the holes with a small stick. The projects in this book use the simpler, visible doweled joints, the example pictured here shows instead a concealed doweled joint.

SPLINED MITER

A miter joint which is simply glued is sometimes not strong enough for the piece. A splined or keyed miter is used to give extra strength to the joint. A slot is cut with a chisel or with a router to accommodate the key, (also known as a biscuit). The key must be a close fit to ensure gluing will be successful.

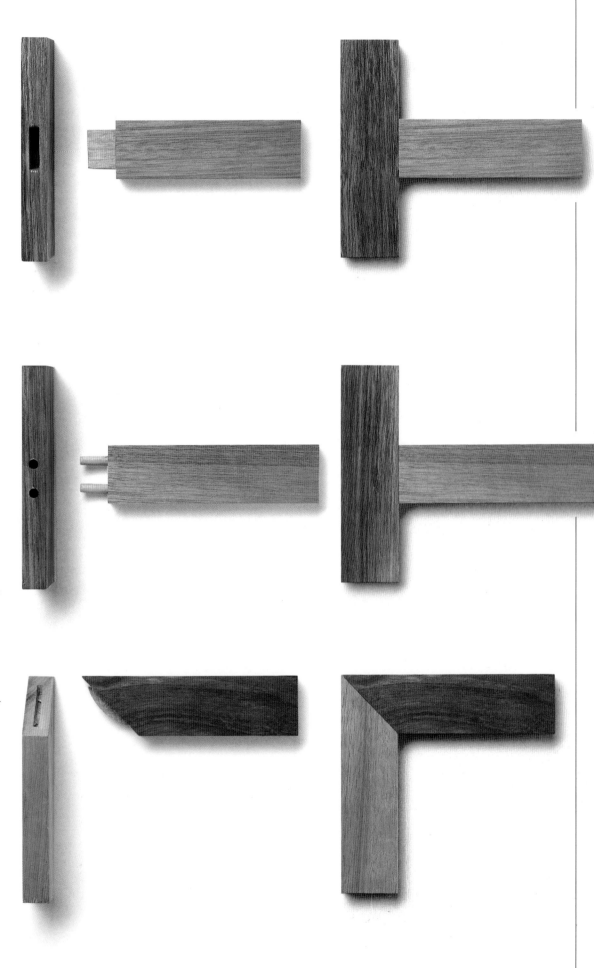

FINISHING TECHNIQUES

PREPARING

In preparation for finishing, erase any remaining pattern tracing lines as they will not come off easily with sanding, particularly in softwoods. When re-using old pieces of timber, ensure any previous layers of paint or finish are properly stripped off. Apply all finishes in a well lit and ventilated area and take care with flammable materials.

TOOLS

It is essential to have the correct tools for the job. If you do not have the power tools for sanding or for spraying on finishes you could borrow or hire them as needed. All tools need to be properly maintained according to the manufacturer's instructions. Always use the safety guards provided with power tools and wear the appropriate safety gear such as ear muffs, face mask and goggles.

Some of the materials needed for surface preparation.

SANDING

If you don't have an orbital sander, then sandpaper and a block will do the job. In most cases sanding is done in stages, starting with a coarse grade of paper first and gradually moving to more refined sandpaper for the final smoothing off. Sandpaper can be wrapped around other tools, such as a screwdriver, for sanding within small holes and other hard to reach areas. A smoothly sanded surface is essential, particularly before proceeding to finish an object by waxing or staining, where the underlying wood will be a feature of the finished piece.

PUTTYING

There will often be areas of your work which need filling or puttying before the piece can be finished. Cracks, imperfections and splits in the wood need to be filled to just above the surface and then left to dry thoroughly before sanding back to finish. If you are planning to finish the timber by applying a stain, oil, wax or paint, read the instructions on the filler before buying it to be sure that it will take the finish you have in mind. It is also a good idea to test it out on a piece of scrap first.

GLUING

When gluing timber together, clamps are used to hold the pieces in place until the glue has dried. The most important requirement for successful gluing is that the join must be kept completely still once glued. Don't clamp the pieces together too tightly as this can cause the timber to buckle or the glue to ooze out and not leave enough to create a firm join. Avoid re-opening a freshly glued join as this can cause the glue to crystalize and may result in a weak join. Use only the recommended quantity of glue and always follow the manufacturer's instructions for use.

SEALING

Sealing is most important on timbers which have an uneven grain, and particularly for hardwoods which are porous, as they are likely to absorb any finishing materials in uneven quantities and this can result in a finish which looks patchy. Check that the sealer will work with the materials used for puttying and with those you will use for the finish.

PAINTING

Painting is an effective finish when you want to achieve a particular decorative style or where the quality of the wood is such that the piece will look and last better painted. As with all finishes, thorough surface preparation is essential. Use a good quality paintbrush, on which the bristles spring back when pressed. Follow the manufacturer's instructions for use, which will be on the paint can label. When painting pieces for use by children, choose a non-toxic paint.

ANTIQUING

Commercial antiquing patinas are available which will give your pieces the appearance of being well used and much loved. (For more details see page 86).

PICKLING

Pickling is used to achieve a whitewash effect on light-colored timbers. (For more details see page 42).

LIMING

A painted on and lightly wiped off finish which adds dimension to a piece. (For more details see page 38).

VARNISHING

Varnish provides one of the longest lasting finishes for wooden pieces but it takes a little more time and skill to apply. It is always applied to a smoothly sanded, sealed surface. The most commonly encountered problem in varnishing is bubbling, which can be avoided by stirring the varnish very slowly to avoid creating bubbles and by applying the varnish with light, smooth strokes of the brush. The piece should be left to dry in a dust-free environment for the time specified by the manufacturer. Fine sanding can be carried out between coats to ensure a very smooth and glossy look to the final finish. After sanding, use a tack cloth to wipe the surface clean of dust, before applying the next coat of varnish.

LACQUERING

Lacquer is the name for the traditional Chinese finish which is made from the sap of the *lac* tree. A similar product is made in Japan from the sap of the *urushi* tree. Varnish is the European and American equivalent of lacquer and is made from resins and turpentine.

You will need clean brushes or cloths to apply the finishes.

WAXING

There are various types of waxes commercially available in the form of pastes, liquids and sprays. Wax is applied for protection after the finish has dried. It is important to read the manufacturer's instructions regarding choosing a wax which corresponds to the finish you have used and to follow the directions for use.

STAINING

Stains are colored liquids applied to the finished piece to alter the natural color of the wood. The final color achieved will depend on the type of wood. It is important to use a clean brush or cloth when applying a stain and to carefully follow the manufacturer's directions for use.

CATALOG OF CRAFT TIMBERS

This selection of timbers shows those which have been used in the projects throughout the book, plus a variety of commercially harvested timbers that may be used as substitutes. (Refer to page 148 for more details.) Your local lumber yard will be able to advise you if you are uncertain which timber to purchase. These timbers are generally available in most comprehensive lumber stores.

AMERICAN WHITE ASH
Gray to brown straight grained, coarse textured hardwood used for tools, utensils, handles and sporting goods.
North America, Europe, Japan

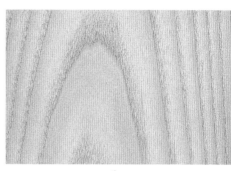

ASH
White, straight grained, hardwood with conspicuous growth rings used for sporting goods, furniture and handles.
Europe, North America, Japan, Australia

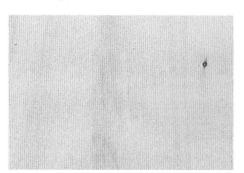

ASPEN/POPLAR
Cream white to pale beige, straight grained but woolly hardwood used for match sticks and furniture.
North America, Europe

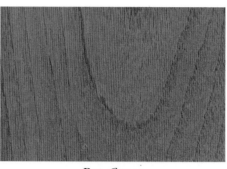

RED CEDAR
Pale to dark red, coarse textured hardwood with straight grain used for furniture.
Australia, Papua New Guinea, South East Asia, India

BALSA
White with pinkish tinge, soft, velvet-like straight grained, light-weight hardwood, used for insulation and models.
Tropical America, Papua New Guinea

BRAZILIAN MAHOGANY
Yellow to red-brown hardwood, moderately fine texture and variable grain, used for furniture and carving.
South America

CHERRY/MYRTLE
Pale pinkish brown, fine textured, straight grained decorative hardwood used for furniture and paneling.
Europe, Asia, Central America

EUROPEAN BEECH
White or pale brown, fine, even, straight grained hardwood used for furniture, stairs and flooring.
Europe, Japan, North America

JAPANESE OAK
Yellowish brown hardwood with moderately coarse texture and straight grain, used for furniture, panels, and veneer.
Japan

JELUTONG
Creamy, fine textured, even grained hardwood used for pattern making, carving, plywood and door core stock.
Malaysia, Indonesia

MAPLE/SYCAMORE
Pale yellow, high density, fine textured, scratch resistant hardwood used for flooring, utensils and musical instruments.
Europe, North America, Japan

MERANTI (PACIFIC MAPLE)
Pale yellow to yellow-brown hardwood, even, coarse texture, mainly straight grain, used for furniture and internal moldings.
Indonesia, Philippines

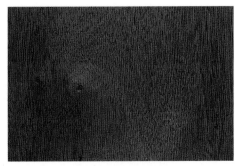

ROSE MAHOGANY
Reddish brown, fine and uniform textured, interlocked grain hardwood used for furniture and paneling.
Australia

SEN
White and pale gray-brown hardwood, straight grain and uneven medium texture used for furniture.
Japan

TASMANIAN BLACKWOOD
Gold to chocolate brown, straight grain hardwood with a high natural luster often used for furniture.
Australia

WALNUT
Black-brown to gray-purple hardwood with medium texture and straight to wavy grain used for furniture.
Europe, North and Central America, Australia

WILLOW
White to reddish brown, fast growing hardwood, fine even texture used for clogs and cricket bats.
Europe, Western Asia

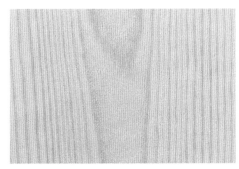

BALTIC PINE
White to pale yellow, medium textured, straight grained softwood used for flooring, cladding and furniture.
Northern Europe

CYPRESS PINE
Pale yellow and variegated brown softwood with a fine, straight grain often used for flooring and frame work.
Australia

KAURI PINE
Pale yellow-brown softwood, fine, even texture and straight grain, used for plywood and furniture.
South East Asia, Papua New Guinea, Philippines

OREGON/DOUGLAS FIR
Pale to medium red-brown, straight grained and resinous softwood used for building, flooring and plywood.
British Columbia, Central America

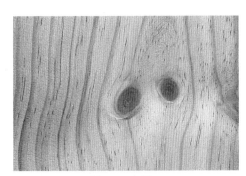

RADIATA PINE
Pale yellow, fine, uneven textured softwood with marked knot and resin characteristic, used for construction, furniture and plywood.
Nth. America, South Africa, New Zealand, Australia

RED PINE
Creamy white to red-brown softwood with straight grain and fine texture used for floors and panels.
Europe, Northern Asia

Alphabetical Summary of Timbers

Hardwoods	Weight	Workability	For use with these projects
American White Ash	heavy	hard	Scandinavian chair, screen, blanket chest, dough bin
Ash	medium - heavy	medium	serving trays, cutlery tray, dough bin, candle box
Aspen/Poplar	light	easy	rocking horse, Mexican sun
Australian Red Cedar	medium	medium	Shaker candlestand, Islamic mirror and table, blanket chest
Balsa	light	easy	rocking horse, Mexican sun
Brazilian Mahogany	medium	easy	dough bin, Shaker candlestand, Islamic table and mirror, Russian toys
Cherry/Myrtle	medium	hard	Shaker candlestand, dough bin, candle box, candleholder, trinket box,
European Beech	heavy	hard	candle box, candleholder, trinket box, Scandinavian chair
Japanese Oak	heavy	hard	Scandinavian chair, screen, food safe, dough bin
Jelutong	light	easy	rocking horse, Mexican sun
Maple/Sycamore	medium - heavy	hard	candle box, candleholder, trinket box, Scandinavian chair
Meranti (Pacific Maple)	light	easy	as listed for the main group of softwoods
Rose Mahogany	medium	easy	Shaker candlestand, Scandinavian chair, blanket chest,
Sen	medium	easy	serving trays, cutlery tray, dough bin, candle box
Tasmanian Blackwood	medium	easy	Shaker candlestand, Scandinavian chair, blanket chest, side table, screen
Walnut	heavy	medium	Shaker candlestand, Scandinavian chair, blanket chest, side table, screen
Willow	light	easy	rocking horse, Mexican sun, cutlery tray, candleholder

Softwoods	Weight	Workability	
Baltic Pine	light	easy	wall cabinet, cutlery tray, grape basket, serving trays
Cypress Pine	heavy	hard	Scandinavian chair, blanket chest
Kauri Pine	light	easy	Islamic mirror and table, dough bin, Scandinavian chair
Oregon/Douglas Fir	light	easy	and wall cabinet, grape picker, side table, trinket box,
Radiata Pine	light	easy	candleholder, blanket chest, candle box, Russian toys,
Red Pine	light	easy	serving trays, cutlery tray, food safe

Metric Conversion Chart

All the projects in this book can be made using either metric or imperial units and both measurements are given in the text thoughout. All conversions are approximate and the dimensions used in the projects can be scaled up or down to suit your own requirements.

However, unless you are an experienced woodworker it may be advisable to allow a little extra in the measurements until you are sure just how the various parts of a project will fit together. At that point you will be able to adjust the size of the component parts to ensure that you have a good fit.

MM	INCHES	CM	FEET	METRES	YARDS
6	1/4	30	1	0.91	1
10	3/8	46	1½	1.38	1½
13	1/2	61	2	1.83	2
16	5/8	76	2½	2.29	2½
19	3/4	91	3	2.74	3
22	7/8	107	3½	3.21	3½
25	1	122	4	3.66	4

Using the Cutting List

The cutting list, which begins on the facing page, describes the actual sizes of the various pieces that make up each of the finished projects. The actual size is known as the *finished* size. Finished timber is also referred to as *DAR,* which stands for "dressed all round." When you buy wood, in most cases it will not be in the finished size and you will have to cut and plane it to the correct measurements. The finished size is described by listing the cross section first, then the length, and finally the number of pieces required.

For example:

$3^{15}/_{16}$ x 2 x 24 / 2 (100 x 50 x 600 / 2)

Means:

Two pieces of wood each $3^{15}/_{16}$ (100 mm) wide by 2 inches (50 mm) deep and $23^5/_8$ (600 mm) long.

platform

saddle: 3⁹/₁₆ x ¹/₁₆ x 4³/₄
(90 x 1 x 120)

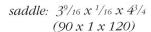

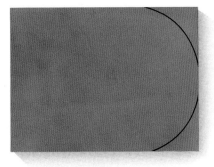

head & neck: 6⁵/₁₆ x 3 x 1¹/₂ / 1
(160 x 75 x 38 / 1)

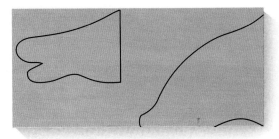

body: 2⁹/₁₆ x 2 x 9⁷/₈ / 1
(65 x 50 x 250 / 1)

saddle seat back

rockers, legs, end spacers,
platform & saddle seat back:
3¹⁵/₁₆ x ³/₈ x 23⁵/₈ / 2
(100 x 10 x 600 / 2)

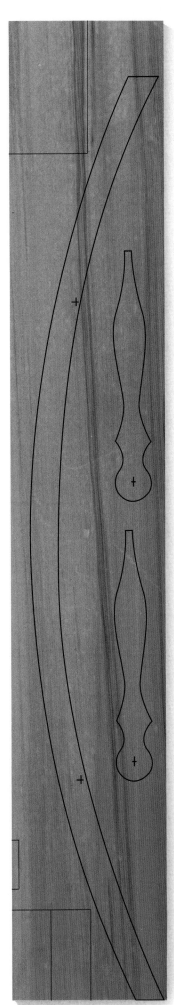

end spacers

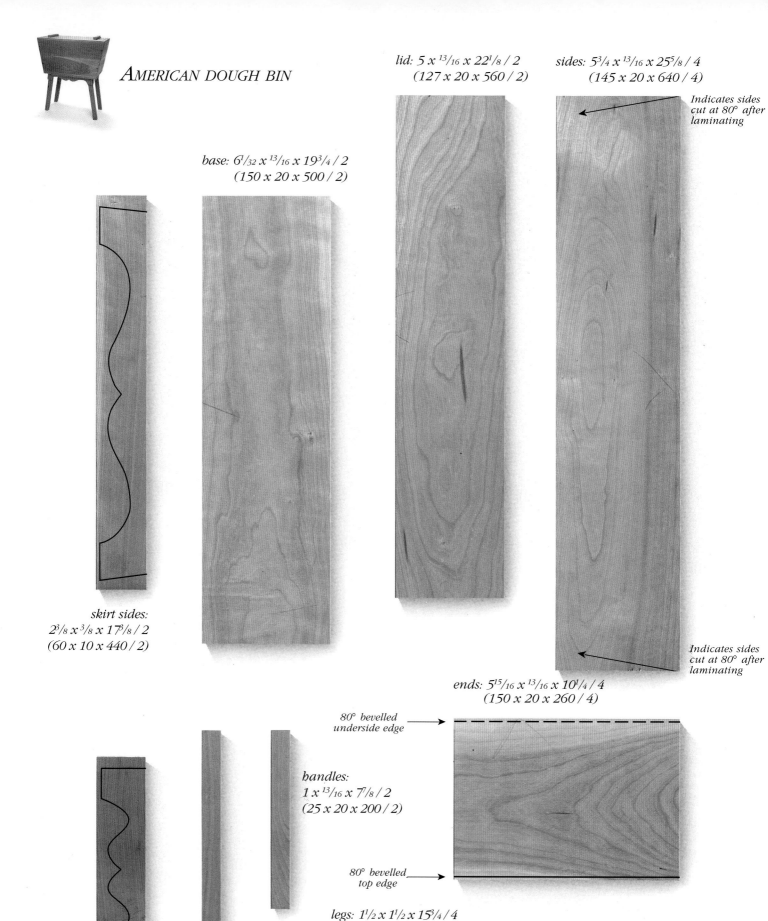

AMERICAN DOUGH BIN

lid: 5 x ¹³/₁₆ x 22¹/₈ / 2
(127 x 20 x 560 / 2)

sides: 5³/₄ x ¹³/₁₆ x 25⁵/₈ / 4
(145 x 20 x 640 / 4)

Indicates sides
cut at 80° after
laminating

base: 6¹/₃₂ x ¹³/₁₆ x 19³/₄ / 2
(150 x 20 x 500 / 2)

Indicates sides
cut at 80° after
laminating

skirt sides:
2³/₈ x ³/₈ x 17³/₈ / 2
(60 x 10 x 440 / 2)

ends: 5¹⁵/₁₆ x ¹³/₁₆ x 10¹/₄ / 4
(150 x 20 x 260 / 4)

80° bevelled
underside edge

handles:
1 x ¹³/₁₆ x 7⁷/₈ / 2
(25 x 20 x 200 / 2)

80° bevelled
top edge

legs: 1¹/₂ x 1¹/₂ x 15³/₄ / 4
(38 x 38 x 400 / 4)

80° bevel

80° bevel

skirt ends:
2³/₈ x ¹³/₁₆ x 9⁷/₈ / 2
(60 x 20 x 250 / 2)

cleats:
1 x ¹³/₁₆ x 11¹/₁₆ / 4
(25 x 20 x 280 / 4)

150

SHAKER CANDLESTAND

end plate:
$3^{3}/_{8} x {}^{3}/_{16} x 2^{15}/_{16} / 1$
$(85 x 5 x 75 / 1)$

pedestal:
$2^{15}/_{16} x 2^{15}/_{16} x 20^{6}/_{8} / 1$
$(75 x 75 x 525 / 1)$

top: $9^{7}/_{8} x 1 x 19^{3}/_{4} / 2$
$(250 x 25 x 500 / 2)$ (only half pattern shown)

doughnut: $5^{15}/_{16} x 1 x 5^{15}/_{16} / 1$
$(150 x 25 x 150 / 1$

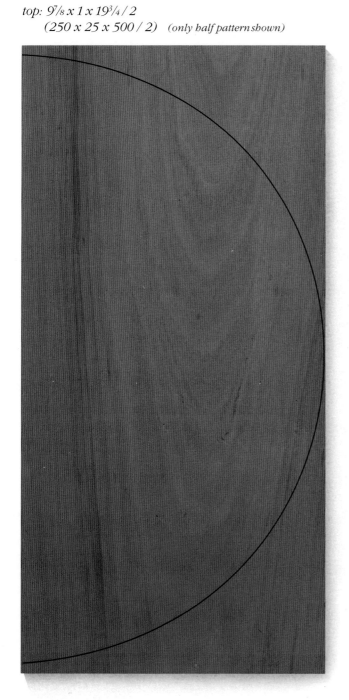

legs: $5^{1}/_{2} x 1^{3}/_{8} x 12^{3}/_{8} / 3$
$(140 x 30 x 310 / 3)$

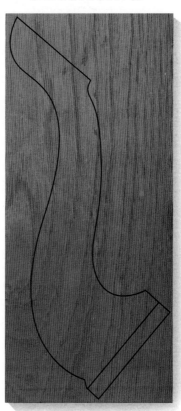

SHAKER BOX

box side:
$3^3/_8$ x $^1/_4$ x $22^{11}/_{16}$ / 1
(85 x 3 x 575 / 1)

lid:
1 x $23^1/_8$ / 1
(25 x 585 / 1)

inner strip:
$^5/_{16}$ x $23^1/_8$ / 1
8 x 585 / 1

top and base: $5^1/_2$ x $7^1/_2$ / 2
(140 x 190 / 2)

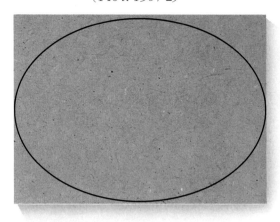

laminates for top and base: $5^1/_2$ x $7^1/_2$ / 4
(140 x 190 / 4)

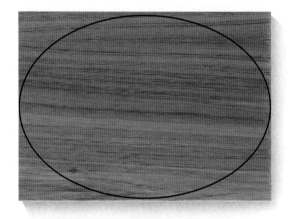

formers: $5^1/_2$ x $2^{15}/_{16}$ x $7^1/_2$ / 2
(140 x 75 x 190 / 2)

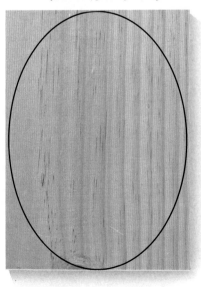

SCANDINAVIAN
WALL CUPBOARD

shelves: $3^{15}/_{16}$ x $^1/_2$ x $11^{13}/_{16}$ / 2 (100 x 12 x 300 / 2)

door stile:
$1^9/_{16}$ x $^{13}/_{16}$ x $10^7/_{16}$ / 2
(40 x 20 x 265 / 2)

top and base: $4^3/_4$ x $^{13}/_{16}$ x $11^{13}/_{16}$ / 2 (120 x 20 x 300 / 2)

supports:
$^{13}/_{16}$ x $^1/_2$ x $3^{15}/_{16}$ / 4
(20 x 12 x 100 / 4)

pediment: $2^3/_4$ x $^{13}/_{16}$ x $13^5/_8$ / 1 (70 x 20 x 345 / 1)

door rail:
$1^9/_{16}$ x $^{13}/_{16}$ x $17^3/_4$ / 2
(40 x 20 x 450 / 2)

side panels: $4^3/_4$ x $^{13}/_{16}$ x $17^3/_4$ / 2 (120 x 20 x 450 / 2)

V-joint backing: $3^{15}/_{16}$ x $^1/_2$ x $16^9/_{16}$ / 3 (100 x 12 x 420 / 3)

door panel: $5^3/_4$ x $^3/_8$ x $15^3/_4$ / 2 (145 x 10 x 400 / 2) (only half pattern shown)

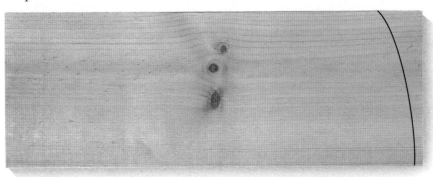

SCANDINAVIAN CHAIR

NOTE: The six small wedges used to secure the backrest and legs can be taken from offcuts.

legs:
$1^{13}/_{16}$ x $1^{13}/_{16}$ x 79 / 1
(45 x 45 x 2000 / 1)

The tapering for one leg top

seat: $8^5/_{16}$ x $1^3/_8$ x $17^3/_4$ / 2
(210 x 30 x 450 / 2)   (shows 2 equal width pieces laminated)

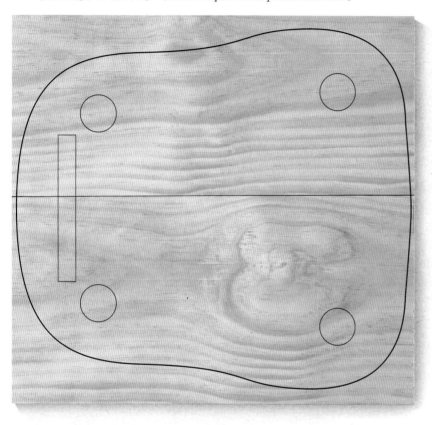

NOTE: The plan shown is for the top of the seat. The mortise and front holes are at 80° angles and the back holes at 70° to allow for the slope of the backrest and the splaying of the legs.

support pieces:
$1^3/_8$ x $5/_8$ x $5^{15}/_{16}$ / 2
(30 x 15 x 150 / 2)

NOTE: The chair backrest is at an 80° angle, so cut this tenon accordingly

backrest: $8^5/_{16}$ x $1^3/_8$ x $25^5/_8$ / 1
(210 x 30 x 650 / 1)

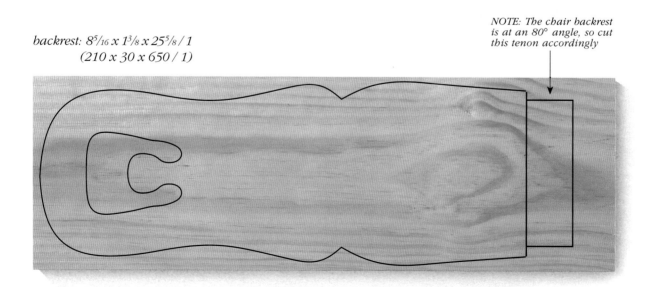

FRENCH GRAPE BASKET

cane handle:
$^{13}/_{16}$ *x 39$^1/_2$/ 1*
(20 x 1000 / 1)

sides: 5$^{15}/_{16}$ x $^3/_8$ x 17$^3/_4$ / 2 (150 x 10 x 450 / 2)

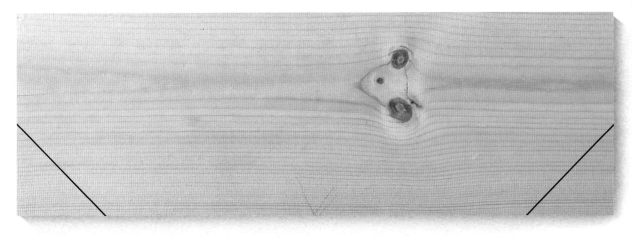

base: 5$^{15}/_{16}$ x $^3/_8$ x 11$^{13}/_{16}$ / 2
(150 x 10 x 300 / 2)

lower ends: 4$^{15}/_{16}$ x $^3/_8$ x 11$^{13}/_{16}$ / 2
(125 x 10 x 300 / 2)

upper ends: 2$^{15}/_{16}$ x $^3/_8$ x 11$^{13}/_{16}$ / 2
(75 x 10 x 300 / 2)

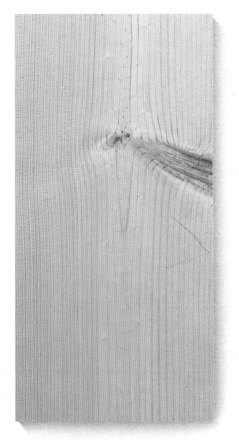
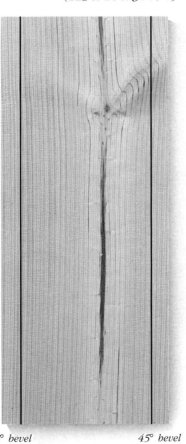

45° bevel   *45° bevel*

155

FRENCH PROVINCIAL TABLE

top: $14^1/_4$ x 1 x $47^3/_8$ / 1 (360 x 25 x 1200 / 1)

side rails:
$4^3/_4$ x 1 x $7^1/_2$ / 2
(120 x 25 x 190 / 2)

front & back rail:
$4^3/_4$ x 1 x $39^1/_2$ / 2
(120 x 25 x 1000 / 2)

legs:
$2^9/_{16}$ x $2^9/_{16}$ x $28^3/_8$ / 4
(65 x 65 x 720 / 4)

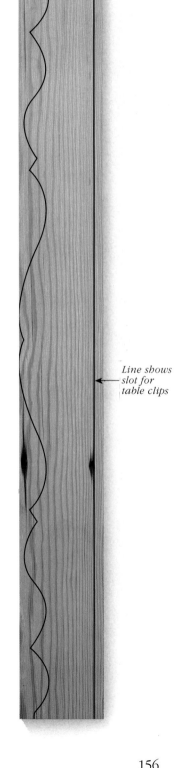

Line shows
slot for
table clips

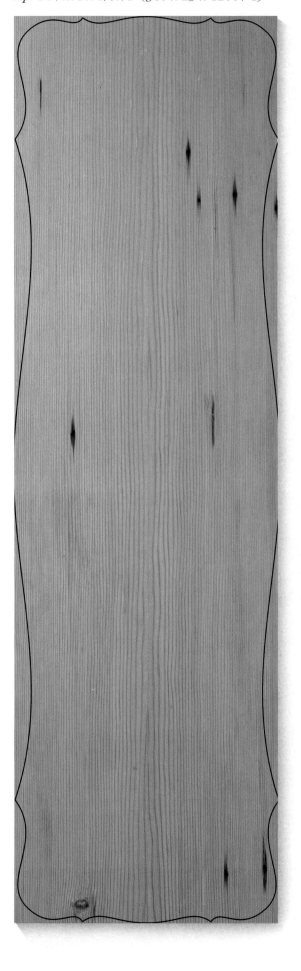

TREEN CANDLEHOLDER

$4^9/_{16} x ^1/_2 x 22^1/_8 / 1$
$(116 x 12 x 560 / 1)$

TREEN TRINKET BOX

lid sides & ends:
$^{13}/_{16}$ x $^1/_2$ x $7^1/_8$ / 2
(20 x 12 x 180 / 2)

box sides & ends:
$1^9/_{16}$ x $^1/_2$ x $7^1/_8$ / 2
(39 x 12 x 180 / 2)

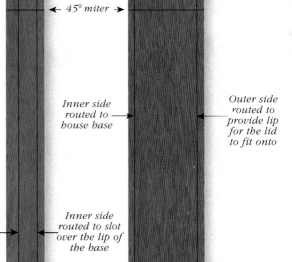

← 45° miter →

NOTE:
Plans are
shown for one
side and one
end of both top
and base.

Inner side
routed to
house base

Outer side
routed to
provide lip
for the lid
to fit onto

Inner side
routed to
house inlay
top

Inner side
routed to slot
over the lip of
the base

inlay: $3^1/_8$ x $^1/_4$ x $6^1/_2$ / 1 (80 x 6 x 165 / 1)

← 45° miter →

← 45° miter →

base: $3^1/_8$ x $^1/_8$ x $6^1/_2$ / 1 (80 x 3 x 165 / 1)

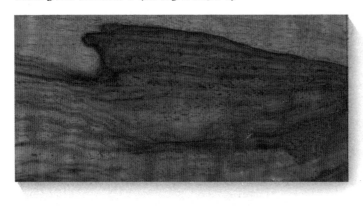

← 45° miter →

lid:
$5^{1}/_{8} x {}^{13}/_{16} x 36^{9}/_{16} / 4$
$(130 x 20 x 930 / 4)$

front & back:
$4^{3}/_{4} x {}^{13}/_{16} x 35 / 8$
$(120 x 20 x 890 / 8)$

ends: $4^{3}/_{4} x {}^{13}/_{16} x 23^{5}/_{8} / 8$
$(120 x 20 x 600 / 8)$
(two pieces shown)

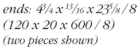

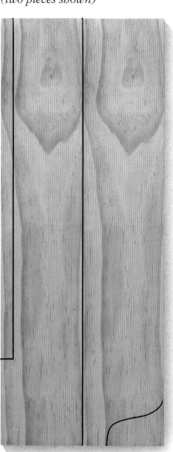

cleats:
$^{13}/_{16} x {}^{13}/_{16} x 33^{1}/_{2} / 2$
$(20 x 20 x 850 / 2)$

dowel rod:
$^{5}/_{16} x 70^{7}/_{8} / 2$
$(8 x 1800 / 2)$

base: $5^{1}/_{2} x {}^{1}/_{2} x 17^{5}/_{16} / 6$ $(140 x 12 x 440 / 6)$

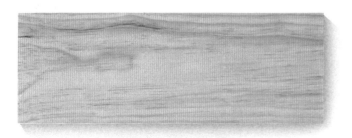

GERMAN CANDLE BOX

sawn to create 2 sides & 2 ends:
$3^{15}/_{16} \times {}^{1}/_{2} \times 33^{1}/_{2} / 1$ (100 x 12 x 850 / 1)

NOTE: Routed slots and rabbets shown on sides and ends are all $^{1}/_{4} \times {}^{1}/_{4}$ inch (6 x 6 mm).

lid handle: $5 \times {}^{1}/_{2} \times {}^{11}/_{16} / 1$ (126 x 12 x 17 / 1)

NOTE: Rabbets shown on lid handle, lid and base are all $^{1}/_{4}$ inch (6 mm) wide and $^{5}/_{16}$ inch (7.5 mm) deep.

lid & base: $4^{7}/_{8} \times {}^{1}/_{2} \times 22^{11}/_{16} / 1$ (124 x 12 x 572 / 1)

lid & base
(the lid and base are identical, one half is shown fully and the other half runs off the page below)

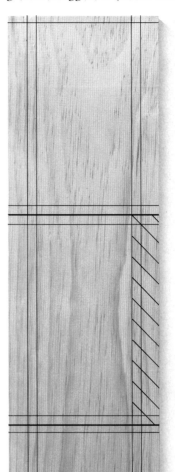

wide end

narrow end
(the hatched section is cut away to accommodate the handle, which could be made from this offcut)

side
(the other identical side runs off the page below)

rods: $1^{11}/_{16}$ x $^{11}/_{16}$ x $12^{13}/_{16}$ / 2 (18 x 18 x 325 / 2) *(both are shown here)*

figures: $3^{15}/_{16}$ x $^{1}/_{4}$ x $15^{3}/_{4}$ / 1
(100 x 6 x 400 / 1)

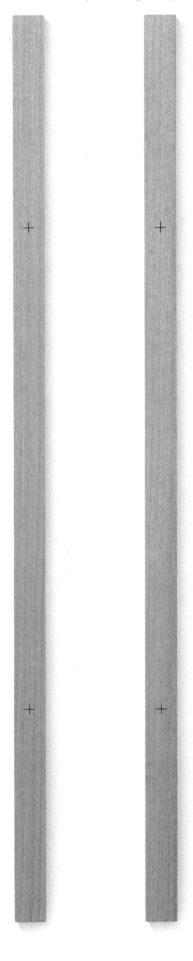

RUSSIAN PECKING HENS

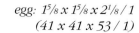
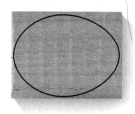

platter: $7^1/_8 x^5/_{16} x 9^7/_8 / 1$
$(180 x 8 x 250 / 1)$

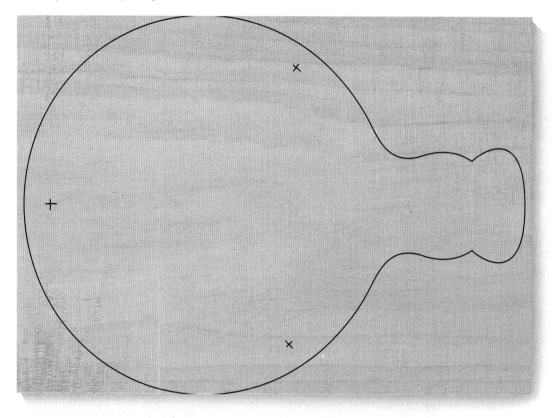

figures: $5 x^1/_4 x 11^{13}/_{16} / 1$
$(126 x 6 x 300 / 1)$

Small rod to make pivot pieces

MEXICAN FRAME

NOTE: The timber shown here is what we used for our project. The idea is to use whatever old timber you have on hand (or can locate) that will be suitable for the size, style and shape of frame you want to make.

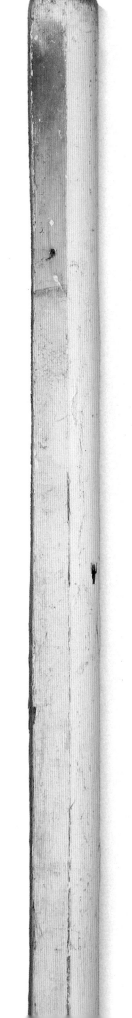

rays: $2^5/_8$ x 1 x 109$^1/_2$ / 1
(66 x 25 x 3000 / 1)

face: $8^{11}/_{16}$ x $1^3/_{16}$ x $8^{11}/_{16}$ / 1
(220 x 30 x 220 / 1)

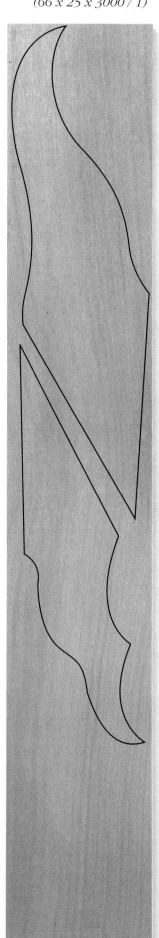

NOTE: There are 2 different "ray" profiles used. For the 6 smaller ones the acute angle where the rays butt is 26° and for the 6 larger ones it is 34°. These angles ensure the rays butt together to make up 360° and form a circle.

FRETWORK MIRROR

dowel: $^3/_8$ x 11$^3/_{16}$ (9 x 300)

top frame: 2$^9/_{16}$ x $^9/_{16}$ x 19$^3/_4$ / 4 (65 x 13 x 500 / 4)

back frame: 3$^3/_{16}$ x $^3/_4$ x 22$^1/_8$ / 4 (80 x 19 x 560 / 4)

fretwork: 16$^3/_{16}$ x $^9/_{16}$ x 23$^5/_8$ / 1 (410 x 13 x 600 / 1)

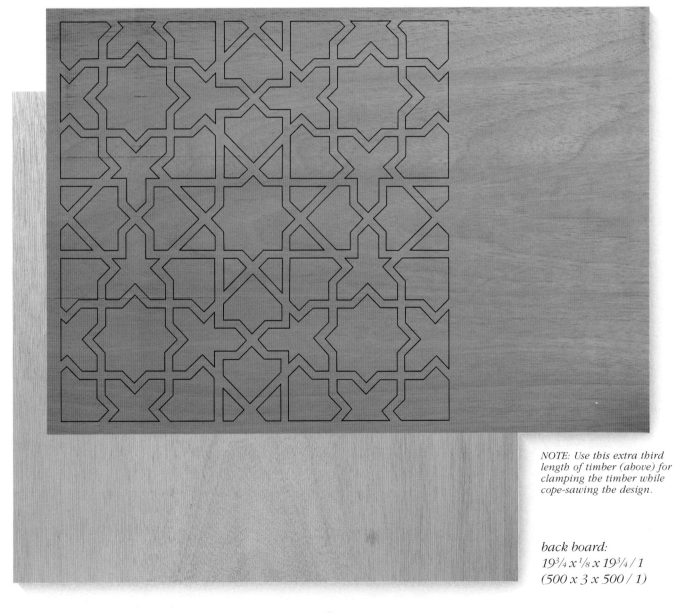

NOTE: Use this extra third length of timber (above) for clamping the timber while cope-sawing the design.

back board:
19$^3/_4$ x $^1/_8$ x 19$^3/_4$ / 1
(500 x 3 x 500 / 1)

FRETWORK TABLE

plywood skirt backing: $2^{15}/_{16}$ x $^1/_{16}$ x $9^7/_{16}$ / 6
(75 x 2 x 240 / 6)

skirts: $3^1/_8$ x $^3/_4$ x $11^1/_{16}$ / 6
(80 x 19 x 280 / 6)

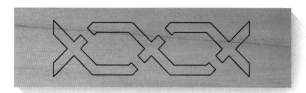

table-top and shelf: $5^1/_2$ x $^3/_4$ x $23^5/_8$ / 8
(140 x 19 x 600 / 8) *(four pieces laminated for each component, inner line denotes shelf)*

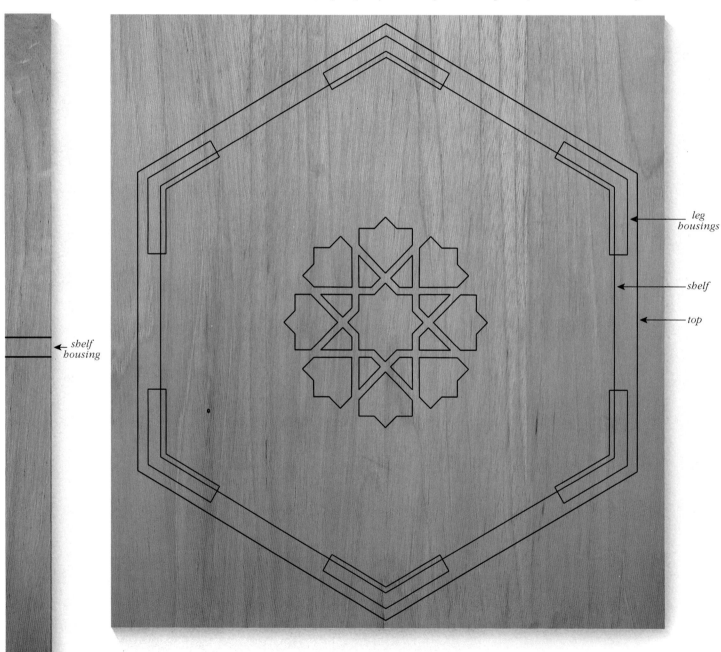

leg housings

shelf

top

← *shelf housing*

legs:
2 x $^3/_4$ x $27^5/_8$ / 12
(50 x 19 x 700 / 12)

Edges: $^{13}/_{16}$ x $^{13}/_{16}$ x $12^1/_4$ / 6
(20 x 20 x 310 / 6)

JAPANESE SERVING TRAYS

base: 13³/₈ x ¹/₄ x 13³/₈ / 3 (340 x 6 x 340 / 3)   *(measurements given to make 3 trays)*

sides: 1¹³/₁₆ x ¹/₂ x 13¹³/₁₆ / 12
(45 x 12 x 350 / 12)

← 45° miter

¹/₄ inch (6 mm)
rabbet routed
to ¹/₈ inch
(3 mm) depth

← 45° miter

JAPANESE SCREEN

frame sides: 2 x ¹³/₁₆ x 65¹/₈ / 6   (50 x 20 x 1650 / 6)   frame top & base: 2 x ¹³/₁₆ x 17³/₄ / 6 (50 x 20 x 450 / 6)

rabbet routed ¹/₂ x ¹/₂ inch (12 x 12 mm)

vertical struts: ¹/₂ x ¹/₂ x 65¹/₈ / 9   (12 x 12 x 1650 / 9)   horiztontal struts: ¹/₂ x ¹/₂ x 17³/₄ / 21 (12 x 12 x 450 / 21)

cover strip sides : ¹³/₁₆ x ¹/₄ x 65¹/₈ / 6 (20 x 6 x 1650 / 6)   cover strip top & base : ¹³/₁₆ x ¹/₄ x 17³/₄ / 6 (20 x 6 x 450 / 6)

(measurements given to make 3 frames for complete screen)

Colonial food safe

base: 1⁹/₁₆ x ¹/₂ x 19³/₄ / 1 (40 x 12 x 500 / 1)

base: 6¹/₈ x ¹/₂ x 19³/₄ / 2 (155 x 12 x 500 / 2)

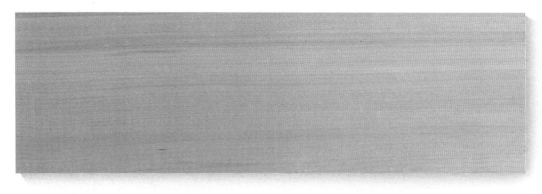

top: 3¹⁵/₁₆ x ¹/₂ x 20¹¹/₁₆ / 1 (100 x 12 x 520 / 1)

top: 6¹/₈ x ¹/₂ x 20¹¹/₁₆ / 2 (155 x 12 x 520 / 2)

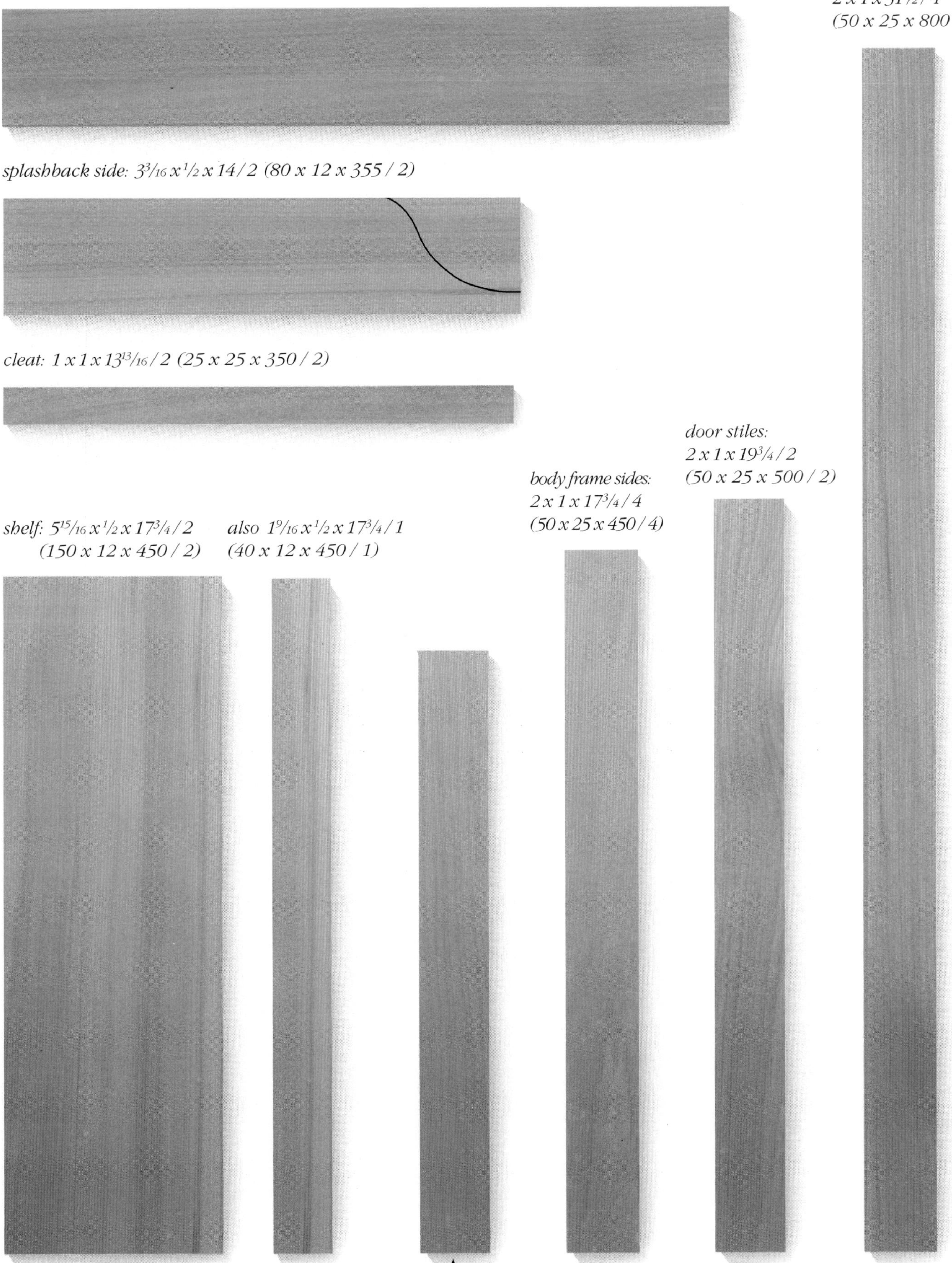

splashback: $3^3/_{16}$ x $^1/_2$ x $19^3/_4$ / 1 (80 x 12 x 500 / 1)

*body frame (legs):
2 x 1 x $31^1/_2$ / 4
(50 x 25 x 800 / 4)*

splashback side: $3^3/_{16}$ x $^1/_2$ x 14 / 2 (80 x 12 x 355 / 2)

cleat: 1 x 1 x $13^{13}/_{16}$ / 2 (25 x 25 x 350 / 2)

*door stiles:
2 x 1 x $19^3/_4$ / 2
(50 x 25 x 500 / 2)*

*body frame sides:
2 x 1 x $17^3/_4$ / 4
(50 x 25 x 450 / 4)*

*shelf: $5^{15}/_{16}$ x $^1/_2$ x $17^3/_4$ / 2
(150 x 12 x 450 / 2)*

*also $1^9/_{16}$ x $^1/_2$ x $17^3/_4$ / 1
(40 x 12 x 450 / 1)*

*body frame (front & back): 2 x 1 x $15^3/_4$ / 4 (50 x 25 x 400 / 4)
&
door rail: 2 x 1 x $15^3/_4$ / 2 (50 x 25 x 400 / 2)*

COLONIAL CUTLERY TRAY

ends: 5¹/₈ x ¹/₂ x 10¹/₄ / 2 (130 x 12 x 260 / 2)

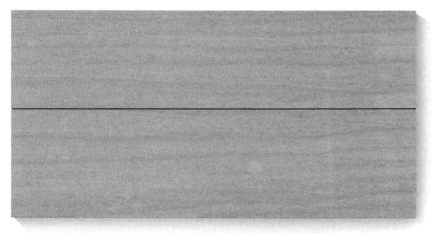

sides: 2¹⁵/₁₆ x ¹/₂ x 15³/₄ / 2 (75 x 12 x 400 / 2)

handle: 4¹⁵/₁₆ x ¹/₂ x 15 / 1 (125 x 12 x 380 / 1)

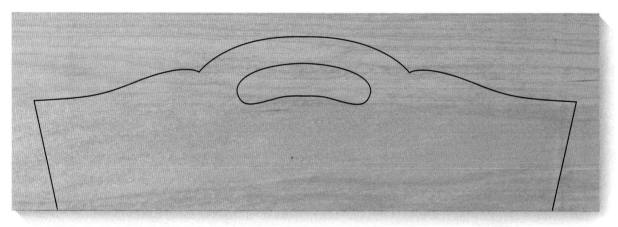

base: 4¹⁵/₁₆ x ¹/₂ x 15 / 2 (125 x 12 x 380 / 2)

GLOSSARY

antiquing: The application of paint and a medium to give a painted piece an aged and mellow appearance.

armoire: A large wardrobe or moveable cupboard, originating in France.

Limed armoire

bar clamp: For holding large pieces of wood or bulky items while gluing.

bevel: An angled edge, formed by planing.

buffer: A scrap of timber used when clamping to prevent surface damage.

burl: A round growth on the trunk of a tree which is prized for its unusual grain and often sliced to make veneer.

butt joint: The simplest method of joining timber by gluing or nailing two square-cut pieces together.

c-clamp: For holding timber together while gluing.

cabriole: A table or chair leg curved in an S-shape.

capping: The horizontal piece of timber, often molded, on top of a piece of furniture.

carpenter's mallet: Used with flat carpenter's chisels.

chamfer: An oblique surface cut on the edge or corner of a board, usually sloping at 45°.

clamp: To attach an object to a firm base while carrying out a task such as planing, sawing, etc. Or to fix glued pieces in position until glue dries.

claw hammer: Hammer with rounded head for hammering in nails and a curved claw for pulling them out.

cleat: A small strip of wood that acts as a support.

clontage: A French provincial method of decorating wood with nail heads.

coffre: A sideboard or cupboard.

coping saw: For cutting out fine shapes.

countersink bit: Used to ream out the top of the hole to fit a countersunk screw head.

countersink: To enlarge the upper section of a screw hole so that the screw head lies flush with the surface.

curved woodcarving gouge: U-shaped blade used for creating sculpted shapes. Woodcarving gouges also come with V-shaped blades. See also veiner.

damage: To purposely mark or dent pieces.

dovetail: A strong decorative joint of mortise and pins shaped like a dove's tail.

Dovetail joint

dowel: A round wooden pin which fits into matching holes in two adjacent pieces of wood to form a joint.

doweling jig: For drilling accurate 90° holes within the timber surface to contain dowels.

dower chest: Domestic storage chests that often formed part of a bride's dowry; the tradition was brought to America by German immigrants.

dressed: Timber which has been prepared with all the surfaces smoothed and so has smaller dimensions than the nominal size, (also called DAR, dressed all round).

dresser: A kitchen sideboard, commonly with a set of shelves for displaying plates.

Federal: American neoclassical style of furniture which often featured the eagle in decoration.

fiberboard: A constructed board of wood fibers bonded together and compressed.

figure: A very distinctive pattern in the grain of timber, which is revealed by cutting through growth rings that are different colors and widths.

file: Used for finer finishing of timber, round files are used for enlarging holes. See also rasp.

finial: A vertical ornament on a chair, headboard, etc.

flat carpenter's chisel: Used for making joins.

food safe: A ventilated cabinet, either on legs or designed for hanging, in which food could be kept safe from insects and animals.

fretwork: Openwork decoration in timber; also known as scrollwork.

Fretwork box

glue: Used for fixing timbers together. See also PVA.

grain: The pattern produced by the growth of the fibers of a tree, which run the length of the tree, and the appearance that characteristically results.

grain painting: Mimicking the grain of an expensive timber by marking patterns in a layer of thickened paint.

hand drill: Used for light drilling such as small holes, or in softwoods.

handsaw: For hand-cutting larger pieces of wood.

hand plane: For creating flat surfaces and edges.

hardwood: Close-grained timber with small pores which comes from broadleaved trees, like oak, cherry and maple.

housing: The space made in one piece of wood for the insertion of another piece.

jigsaw: A narrow saw mounted vertically in a frame and used for cutting curves.

kubbestol: A Scandinavian chair fashioned in one piece from a hollowed log.

lacquer: A natural type of varnish obtained from the sap of a tree, used in Japanese and Chinese woodworking.

laminate: To glue two or more pieces of timber together to form a wider, stronger or thicker piece.

liming: The process of painting wood with a pale wash of color.

Japanese lacquerwork bowls

lit clos: A box bed which was common in the Breton region of France.

marking gauge: Used to set out rabbets and tenons.

marquetry: Inlaid work of different colored woods which are arranged to form a pattern.

mashrabiya: One of the many spellings used to describe Islamic fretwork in screens and balconies, also called meshrebeeyeh, moucharaby, and mushrebiyeh.

matryushka: A series of progressively smaller wooden nesting dolls which originated in Russia.

milk paint: Finish made from skim milk which dried to a brittle finish and washed off easily, it was popular with early American woodworkers.

miter: A true miter is made at a 45° angle.

miter box: Used to hold strips of timber while cutting it to precise angles with a tenon saw.

miter joint: A diagonal joint made by fitting together two pieces of timber to form a 90° corner.

mortise: A cavity in a piece of wood for accommodating a projection in another piece which forms a joint.

molding: A contoured strip of timber often used to decorate the edge or top of a piece of furniture.

netsuke: Miniature carvings from Japan, made from either ivory or wood.

Ebony pokerwork bowls

nominal size: The dimensions of timber as it is bought and before it is dressed. See also dressed.

orbital sander: Power sander, used to sand large flat surfaces to a fine finish.

phillips head screwdriver: Used for screws which have a star shaped slot in the head.

pickling: Whitewashing of raw wood using a pale stain.

plane: To smooth or dress the wood with a plane tool.

plinth: The projecting base of case furniture such as a wardrobe.

plywood: Wood made from thin veneers glued together with the grains at right angles to one another.

pokerwork: Decoration of wood by burning a design into it with a heated iron or point (also called pyrography).

power drill: For heavy drilling especially in hardwood.

power jigsaw: For fast cutting of curved shapes.

profile: To shape timber to the outline of a design, using a jigsaw or other cutting tool.

PVA: Polyvinyl acetate; a strong but slow-drying glue which dries clear.

rail: A strip of wood fixed horizontally for support.

rasp: Tool which can be either curved or flat and is used to roughly shape edges. See also file.

rabbet: A groove or recess made along the edge of a board for decoration or to receive another piece of wood.

rocaille: A shell-shaped motif common in French design.

rosemaling: Norwegian folk painting which typically includes abstract flowers and scrolls.

Rosemaling trinket box

rotary orbital sander: Power sander, used to achieve an extra fine finish.

rout: To hollow out a gouge in a piece of wood.

router: A power tool for making rabbets, gouges or decorative edges on a piece of timber.

sanding block: Useful when sanding flat surfaces, sandpaper is wrapped around the block for an easy grip.

sash clamp: For holding several boards together when laminating.

scaling: The technique of changing the size of a design while retaining its relative dimensions.

schrank: A type of wardrobe traditionally found in Germanic communities

Shaker boxes: Traditional oval shaped boxes famed for their simple design and skillful joining techniques, which originated in the Shaker communities of America.

shellac varnish: Varnish made by dissolving shellac in a solvent.

shoji: A Japanese style of screen or lamp, in which thin paper is fixed over a wooden frame.

sliding bevel: A tool for marking angles which are not 90°. See also try-square.

slot screwdriver: Used for screws which have a straight line slot in the head.

Shoji lamp

softwood: Timber with large open grain and no pores, from evergreen trees which have needles instead of leaves, such as pine and fir trees. Generally much easier to work with for cutting and carving than hardwood.

solvent: Liquid for dissolving paints, varnishes, etc.

spade bit: For use with a power drill for drilling out larger diameter holes.

spindle: A rounded wooden rod that has been turned on a lathe; often used in chair backs, legs, etc.

splashboard: The vertical board backing a bench or cupboard which prevents spillage.

spline: A narrow, thin strip of wood which can be used like dowel to secure a mitered joint.

spokeshave: A cutting tool with an adjustable blade between two handles, used for dressing and forming curved edges.

stile: A bar of wood fixed vertically in a frame.

swallowtail joint: A Shaker joint of swallowtail shaped plywood.

tack hammer: For hammering in tacks and panel pins, particularly in upholstery and on smaller jobs.

tenon: A projection fashioned on the end of a piece of wood for insertion into a cavity or mortise cut in another piece.

tenon saw: For cutting angles and tenons. Used with a miter box (also called a back saw).

tin snips: A tool for making cuts in pieces of metal.

Swallowtail joints

tongue in groove joint: A joint formed by connecting one board with a tongue along an edge and another with a corresponding groove along its edge.

transfer paper: A type of paper coated on one side and used for transferring designs.

Treen: The British name for small wooden utensils, generally made from a single piece of timber.

try-square: Also called a set square, used for marking 90° angles for cutting. See also sliding bevel.

twist drill bit: Standard, high speed bit for use on hand or power drills in wood or metal.

v-shaped woodcarving gouge: Used for doing incised line carving, particularly for creating lettering and borders, gouges also come with curved U-shaped blades.

v-joint backing: Backing board which is bought with a chamfer already fashioned along one or more edges.

varnish: A synthetic coating made of a resin and a solvent and used for finishing.

veiner: Small gouge used for carving fine lines.

veneer: Thin sheets of timber used for decorative purposes.

whirligig: A type of whimsical wind toy which developed in rural America.

Windsor chair: A wooden chair with spindle back and outward-pointing legs, which came originally from the town of Windsor in Britain.

woodcarver's mallet: Wooden mallet used when working with woodcarving gouges.

Woodcarver's mallet and a curved woodcarving gouge

173

CONTRIBUTORS

Neil Alleyn is a professional woodworker based in the mountains near Sydney. He has a particular interest in Japanese woodcraft but successfully turns his hand to a wide variety of styles and techniques.

Pia Bartlett is a Danish woodcraft teacher who studied cabinet-making at the Richards School, and interior and furniture design at the School of Interior Design, both in Copenhagen. Currently she manages the wood workshops of a Steiner school.

Kai Broderix qualified as a Master of Carpentry and Joinery in Germany. He now works as a designer and maker of handcrafted furniture at The Federation Joinery in Sydney, Australia.

Graham Bull is self-taught in woodcarving and dedicates much of his time to teaching the craft to others through his successful Sydney business, Whistlewood. He also specializes in the production of fine hand tools made from Australian desert hardwoods.

Jean-Cristophe Burckhardt studied art in Italy. He now operates a cabinet-making and antique restoration business, Wood Made, from Mittagong in Australia, and specializes in French provincial furniture.

Serge Couturier has a wide experience in decoration and regularly contributes to radio reports on the subject. He now operates his own business, Motif Serge Couturier, which specializes in fantasy finishes.

Brian Eves is an expert in the construction of Shaker boxes, and his work is in great demand. He works from the north coast of New South Wales in Australia.

Poul Erik Hvidkjaer was born in Denmark and now works as a woodworker, photographer, and also as a teacher of art and craft.

Thomas Moser specializes in handcrafted furniture, particularly in the Shaker style, using solid American hardwoods. He has won numerous design awards.

Yoshinobu Noai was trained in traditional Japanese woodcraft by the Japan Decorative Arts Association at the Kyushi Folk Art Village.

Martina Rienzner undertook a traditional apprenticeship with Franz Zacherl in Munich and studied at the Munich Woodcraft Institute. She operates a woodwork business working to the highest standards of the craft.

Noek Witzand trained in Holland and worked in Norway on traditional boats. He now specializes in modern furniture in his business 'Red Herring Design.'

INDEX